Fresh Ways with
Hors-d'Oeuvre

TIME-LIFE BOOKS

EUROPEAN EDITOR: Ellen Phillips
Design Director: Ed Skyner
Director of Editorial Resources: Samantha Hill
Chief Sub-Editor: Ilse Gray

HEALTHY HOME COOKING

SERIES DIRECTOR: Jackie Matthews
Picture Editor: Mark Karras
Studio Stylist: Liz Hodgson
Editorial Assistant: Eugénie Romer

Editorial Staff for *Fresh Ways with Hors-d'Oeuvre*
Editor: Ellen Galford
Researcher: Ellen Dupont
Designer: Lynne Brown
Sub-Editor: Wendy Gibbons

Editorial Production for the Series:
Chief: Maureen Kelly
Assistant: Deborah Fulham
Editorial Department: Theresa John, Debra Lelliott

THE CONTRIBUTORS

PAT ALBUREY is a home economist with a wide experience of preparing foods for photography, teaching cookery and creating recipes. She has written a number of cookery books and was the studio consultant for the Time-Life series *The Good Cook.*

CAROLE HANDSLIP is a cookery writer and broadcaster with a particular interest in healthy eating; the books she has written include, *Wholefood Cookery* and *Vegetarian Cookery.* She has taught at the Cordon Bleu Cookery School in London.

NORMA MACMILLAN has written several cookery books and edited many others. She has worked on various cookery publications, including *Grand Diplôme* and *Supercook.*

NIGEL SLATER learnt cooking in Paris and in English hotels and restaurants. He is a regular contributor to food magazines.

HILARY WALDEN is a food technologist. She has written numerous books and articles on all aspects of cookery.

The following also contributed recipes to this volume:
Joanna Blythman, Maddalena Bonino, Jo Chalmers, Carole Clements, Sylvija Davidson, Graeme Gore-Rowe, Antony Kwok, Cecilia Norman, Lynn Rutherford, Lorna Walker.

THE COOKS

The recipes in this book were cooked for photography by Pat Alburey, Jacki Baxter, Allyson Birch, Jill Eggleton, Carole Handslip, Antony Kwok, Dolly Meers, Lynn Rutherford, Nigel Slater. *Studio assistant:* Rita Walters.

NUTRITION CONSULTANT

PATRICIA JUDD trained as a dietician and worked in hospital practice before returning to university to obtain her MSc and PhD degrees. Since then she has lectured in Nutrition and Dietetics at London University.

Nutritional analyses for *Fresh Ways with Hors-d'Oeuvre* were derived from McCance and Widdowson's *The Composition of Food* by A.A. Paul and D.A.T. Southgate, and other current data.

This volume is one of a series of illustrated cookery books that emphasize the preparation of healthy dishes for today's weight-conscious, nutrition-minded eaters.

Fresh Ways with Hors-d'Oeuvre

BY

THE EDITORS OF TIME-LIFE BOOKS

TIME-LIFE BOOKS/AMSTERDAM

Contents

Pickled Peppers with Mussels

Okra Stuffed with Indian Spices

Minted Broccoli and Cauliflower

Salmon-Filled Choux Buns

Scorzonera with Walnuts and Chervil

3 *Hors-d'Oeuvre in the Microwave* . 131

Warm Skate Salad with Red Pepper Vinaigrette

Auspicious Beginnings

To the first course in a menu falls the happy task of enticement. Like a musical overture, an hors-d'oeuvre heightens expectations and sets the stage for what is to follow. Whatever tempting form an hors-d'oeuvre takes — barbecued seafood, savoury tartlets or a layered terrine of many hues — it gives pleasure in itself, yet stimulates the appetite instead of sating it.

Such delights need not be restricted to dinner parties or grand occasions. For an ordinary family meal, a plate of raw vegetables encircling a creamy dip, or a piping-hot portion of pasta, makes a welcome start and, what is more, a healthy one. For the good news is that none of the 123 hors-d'oeuvre in this book, from the simplest to the most elaborate, is unworthy of a place in a healthy diet.

The recipes in this volume were developed in the Healthy Home Cooking test kitchens in accordance with established nutritional guidelines. It is acknowledged that foods that are high in saturated fats,

beginning of a meal to whet the appetite. Greater precision is impossible, for these so-called small dishes embrace the entire culinary universe. Indeed, the making of hors-d'oeuvre is cookery in microcosm. Every cooking method is called upon and every class of ingredient, from the humblest root vegetables to the choicest seafoods to the most exotic spices, has its part to play.

The recipes here indicate the breadth of the subject. Divided into three chapters, covering cold, hot and microwaved hors-d'oeuvre, and grouped within these sections according to their principal ingredients, they demonstrate a remarkable variety of possible first courses: simple and elaborate salads; a dozen different stuffed vegetables, ranging from artichokes to okra; moulded aspics, aromatic stews, roulades, fresh fish and shellfish prepared in over 30 ways; crêpes, croustades and pastry cases concealing all manner of delicacies; cold meats with robust dressings; purées heady with fresh herbs and garlic; kebabs, quenelles, timbales and spicy meatballs; pasta and pulses; rice and other grains in many guises.

if consumed in excess, may trigger an increase in blood cholesterol, implicated in the development of heart disease. The effects of salt on health are still a matter of debate, but the sodium in salt is thought to contribute to high blood pressure in susceptible people. A certain amount of salt is essential, but most people, especially those who consume a high proportion of processed foods, take in far more salt than their bodies need.

In most of the recipes that follow, one serving of average size contains no more than 250 calories, 6 to 9 g of fat — of which only 3 g or less are saturated fat — 75 mg of cholesterol, and 400 mg of sodium. A few of the hors-d'oeuvre, appropriate for special occasions that merit a little self-indulgence, exceed these limits. The majority fall well below, thus leaving plenty of scope for planning the remaining courses.

Hors-d'oeuvre, literally, means "outside the work" — an extra dish peripheral to the main business of the meal. In 18th-century aristocratic France, the term described something eaten away from the dining table, or consumed as a diversion from the extravagant assemblages set before the guests. In modern usage, an hors-d'oeuvre is defined as a small dish served at the

A new style of cooking

But one common approach underlies this diversity. All these recipes express a new philosophy of cooking, based on the conviction that it is possible to eat well and still eat wisely. The emphasis is on fresh foods, chosen from those richest in nutritional benefits, and cooked in ways that preserve their goodness without undue reliance on saturated fats, cholesterol and salt.

Flavours are clean and vibrant. Natural piquancy or intrinsic sweetness is heightened by marination in lively mixtures of fruit juices, vinegars, aromatic vegetables, wines and spices, and by the liberal addition of the fresh herbs now available in ever-wider varieties. Basil, for example, was once largely restricted to those lucky enough to live in sunny climates; now several different types, from the tiny peppery leaves of bush basil to the large, decorative opal basil, perfume the air of delicatessen shops and specialist greengrocers. Mint, dill, sorrel and a host of others are available even in supermarkets, and are no longer the exclusive preserve of green-fingered rural and suburban gardeners.

When sauces are used, they are based on vegetable or fruit purées, or on cooking juices thickened by reduction rather than by pastes of fats and flour. Creaminess is achieved by the addition of the low-fat soft cheese known as *fromage frais* or of yogurt — either plain low-fat yogurt, or the thick Greek yogurt, often made from goat's or ewe's milk, which contains only half the fat of single cream, and does not separate during cooking.

Dressings for salads are light: fine oils of distinctive flavour, such as virgin olive oil or those derived from hazelnuts or walnuts, need be used only sparingly. They are partnered with vinegars of quality, varied provenance and distinctive aromas: wine, cider, raspberry, and the uniquely sour-sweet balsamic vinegar, aged in casks of chestnut, juniper or mulberry wood.

An emphasis on vegetables and seafood

More than three quarters of the recipes feature vegetables, fish or shellfish. The visual appeal of these ingredients, and their wonderful range of flavours, would be reason enough to choose them as inviting hors-d'oeuvre. But they are also among the most nutritious foods that Nature bestows upon us.

Vegetables are abundantly endowed with vitamins and minerals. Sweet peppers, for instance, are a prime source of the all-important vitamin C, essential for body maintenance and tissue repair; spinach is a generous supplier of iron, carrots a good source of vitamin A. But — with the notable exception of avocados — vegetables possess almost no fat. They are low in calories, generally low in sodium and virtually cholesterol free.

Fish and shellfish are rich in concentrated protein; an average 125 g (4 oz) portion of seafood provides up to half the protein an adult needs in a day. Lean fish, such as cod and sole, are remarkably low in cholesterol and calories; fatty varieties, such as tuna, salmon or mackerel, are still far lower in calories and saturated fat than an equivalent helping of steak. Indeed, current research suggests that the types of fat contained in oily-fleshed fish help prevent the development of certain illnesses, and that many shellfish, especially molluscs such as the mussel, may actually reduce the amount of cholesterol the body absorbs.

Yet healthy hors-d'oeuvre need not be limited to the offerings of the garden or the sea. Meat and poultry confer generous helpings of protein and other nutrients. They warrant a place in your hors-d'oeuvre repertoire as long as you choose lean cuts, scrupulously trim all visible fat, and remove the fat-laden skin of chicken, duck and other birds. For a first course, a small quantity of meat, poultry or game is all that is necessary to provide a stuffing for vegetable cases or pastries, thin slices for a salad, or a forcemeat for meatballs or quenelles. Meat or poultry first courses are particularly suitable for menus with main dishes that are not particularly rich in protein, such as rice pilaffs, certain pasta preparations or vegetable stews.

Hors-d'oeuvre that might have been dismissed, regretfully, as forbidden fruit are redeemed by a few inventive adjustments. Airy, egg-enriched choux dough, for example, which lends itself as well to savoury treatments as it does to patisserie and desserts, is made here with polyunsaturated margarine instead of butter, and less egg yolk than normally required to produce the same amount of dough. The result possesses only half the fat of conventional versions, a considerable reduction in cholesterol, and a texture that is markedly lighter than ordinary choux, but still strong enough to support a filling. Soufflés, normally laden with egg yolks and based on white sauces made with whole milk and butter, rely instead on the support of well-aerated egg whites, low-fat cheeses such as *fromage frais* and vegetable purées. Crêpes are produced with a skimmed-milk batter.

Crisp pastries, to avoid a heavy load of fat, are made of phyllo dough, a Middle-Eastern product now widely available in supermarkets and delicatessens. Its thin, fragile sheets contain no fat, and will dry out and break unless covered with a damp cloth until the moment they are filled, shaped and baked. Although phyllo is traditionally brushed liberally with butter before cooking, here it is baked with little or no lubrication, and still yields light, crackling envelopes for spinach, cheese and shellfish.

Similarly, the sculpted bread cases known as croustades are usually saturated in melted butter before they are crisped in the oven and filled. Yet a light coating of oil gives the same crunchy results with only a fraction of the fat.

Food without frontiers

As well as being healthy, the new cooking is also eclectic. The hors-d'oeuvre recipes in this volume reflect a rich and varied heritage. From Spain come *tapas*, little dishes of sauced or marinated meats and seafood. The *mezze* or first course of the Middle East yields, besides the phyllo-pastry parcels, vegetable purées and spiced chicken wings. The groaning hors-d'oeuvre tables of northern Europe — Scandinavian *smorgasbord* and the *zakuski* of Russia — contribute fish in robust marinades and sauces, as well as blinis, the delicate pancakes that are caviare's time-honoured accompaniment. The delicacies that the Chinese call *dim sum* inspire savoury dumplings.

Although drawing from many ethnic cuisines, the recipes never follow tradition for its own sake. Unorthodox partnerships of flavour abound, the techniques of East and West are juxtaposed. Exotic ingredients are used creatively, to yield scores of truly original and memorable hors-d'oeuvre.

The Key to Better Eating

This book, like others in the Healthy Home Cooking series, presents an analysis of nutrients contained in a single serving of each dish, listed beside the recipe itself, as on the right. Approximate counts for calories, protein, cholesterol, total fat, saturated fat (the kind that increases the body's blood cholesterol) and sodium are given.

Healthy Home Cooking addresses the concerns of today's weight-conscious and health-minded cooks by providing recipes that take into account guidelines set by nutritionists. The secret of eating well has to do with maintaining a balance of foods in the diet; most of us consume too much sugar and salt, too much fat, too many calories, and even more protein than we need. In planning a meal, the cook using the recipes in this book should take into account what the rest of the meal is likely to contribute nutritionally. The cook should also bear in mind that moderation, as in all things, is a good policy when seeking to prepare a balanced meal.

Interpreting the chart

The chart below gives dietary guidelines for healthy men, women and children. Recommended figures vary from country to country, but the principles are the same everywhere. Here, the average daily amounts of calories and protein are from a report by the U.K. Department of Health and Social Security; the maximum advisable daily intake of fat is based on guidelines given by the National Advisory Committee on Nutrition Education (NACNE); those for cholesterol and sodium are based on upper limits suggested by the World Health Organization.

The volumes in the Healthy Home Cooking series do not purport to be diet books, nor do they focus on health foods. Rather, they express a commonsense approach to cooking that uses salt, sugar, cream, butter and oil in moderation while employing other ingredients — herbs, spices, fruits, aromatic vegetables, wines and vinegars — to provide additional flavour and satisfaction.

Calories **180**
Protein **6g**
Cholesterol **70mg**
Total fat **8g**
Saturated fat **2g**
Sodium **70mg**

The recipes make few unusual demands. Naturally they call for fresh ingredients, offering substitutes when these are unavailable. (The substitute is not calculated in the nutrient analysis, however.) Most of the recipe ingredients can be found in any well-stocked supermarket; the occasional exception can be bought in speciality or ethnic shops.

In Healthy Home Cooking's test kitchens, heavy-bottomed pots and pans are used to guard against foods burning and sticking whenever a small amount of oil is used; non-stick pans are utilized as well. Both safflower oil and virgin olive oil are favoured for sautéing. Safflower oil was chosen because it is the most highly polyunsaturated vegetable fat available in supermarkets, and polyunsaturated fats reduce blood cholesterol; if unobtainable, use sunflower oil, which is also high in polyunsaturated fats. Virgin olive oil is used because it has a fine fruity flavour lacking in the lesser grade known as "pure". In addition, it is — like all olive oil — high in monounsaturated fats, which are thought not to increase blood cholesterol. Virgin and safflower oils can be combined, with olive oil contributing its fruitiness to the safflower oil. When virgin olive oil is unavailable, "pure" may be substituted.

About cooking times

To help the cook plan ahead effectively, Healthy Home Cooking takes time into account in all its recipes. While recognizing that everyone cooks at a different speed, and that stoves and ovens differ in temperatures, the series provides approximate "working" and "total" times for every dish. Working time stands for the minutes actively spent on preparation; total time includes unattended cooking time, as well as any other time devoted to marinating, steeping or soaking ingredients. Since the recipes emphasize fresh foods, they may take a bit longer to prepare than quick and easy dishes that call for canned or packaged products, but the payoff in flavour and often in nutrition should compensate for the little extra time involved.

Recommended Dietary Guidelines

		Average Daily Intake		Maximum Daily Intake			
		CALORIES	PROTEIN grams	CHOLESTEROL milligrams	TOTAL FAT grams	SATURATED FAT grams	SODIUM milligrams
Females	7-8	1900	47	300	80	32	2000*
	9-11	2050	51	300	77	35	2000
	12-17	2150	53	300	81	36	2000
	18-54	2150	54	300	81	36	2000
	54-74	1900	47	300	72	32	2000
Males	7-8	1980	49	300	80	33	2000
	9-11	2280	57	300	77	38	2000
	12-14	2640	66	300	99	44	2000
	15-17	2880	72	300	108	48	2000
	18-34	2900	72	300	109	48	2000
	35-64	2750	69	300	104	35	2000
	65-74	2400	60	300	91	40	2000

* (or 5g salt)

Fish Stock

Makes about 2 litres (3½ pints)
Working time: about 15 minutes
Total time: about 40 minutes

1 kg	lean fish bones, fins and tails discarded, the bones rinsed thoroughly and chopped into large pieces	2 lb
2	onions, thinly sliced	2
2	sticks celery, chopped	2
1	carrot, peeled and thinly sliced	1
½ litre	dry white wine	16 fl oz
2 tbsp	fresh lemon juice	2 tbsp
1	leek (optional), trimmed, split, washed thoroughly to remove all grit, and sliced	1
3	garlic cloves (optional), crushed	3
10	parsley stems	10
3	fresh thyme sprigs, or 1 tsp dried thyme	3
1	bay leaf	1
5	black peppercorns, cracked	5

Put the fish bones, onions, celery, carrot, wine, lemon juice, 2 litres (3½ pints) of water, and the leek and garlic, if you are using them, in a large non-reactive stockpot. Bring the liquid to the boil, then reduce the heat to medium to maintain a strong simmer. Skim off all the scum that rises to the surface.

Add the parsley, thyme, bay leaf and peppercorns. Reduce the heat to medium low and simmer the stock for 20 minutes.

Strain the stock through a fine sieve lined with muslin. Allow the stock to cool before refrigerating or freezing it. The fish stock will keep for three days in the refrigerator or, if it is stored in small, well-sealed freezer containers, it may be kept frozen for as long as two months.

EDITOR'S NOTE: *Because the bones from oilier fish produce a strong flavour, be sure to use only the bones from lean fish. Sole, plaice, turbot and other flat fish are best. Do not include the fish skin; it could discolour the stock.*
The shells from shrimps, prawns and crabs may be added to the stock to give it a pronounced shellfish flavour.

Chicken Stock

Makes 2 to 3 litres (3½ to 5¼ pints)
Working time: about 20 minutes
Total time: about 3 hours

2 to 2.5 kg	uncooked chicken trimmings and bones (preferably wings, necks and backs), the bones cracked with a heavy knife	4 to 5 lb
2	carrots, cut into 1 cm (½ inch) rounds	2
2	sticks celery, cut into 2.5 cm (1 inch) pieces	2
2	large onions, cut in half, one half stuck with 2 cloves	2
2	sprigs fresh thyme, or ½ tsp dried thyme	2
1 or 2	bay leaves	1 or 2
10 to 15	parsley stems	10 to 15
5	black peppercorns	5

Put the trimmings and bones in a heavy stockpot with enough water to cover them by 5 cm (2 inches). Bring the liquid to the boil, skimming off the scum that rises to the surface. Simmer for 10 minutes, skimming and adding a little cold water to help precipitate the scum. Add the vegetables, herbs and peppercorns, and submerge them in the liquid. If necessary, add enough additional water to cover the vegetables or bones. Return to the boil, then lower the heat and simmer for 2 to 3 hours, skimming once more.

Strain the stock and allow it to stand until tepid, then refrigerate it overnight or freeze it long enough for the fat to congeal. Spoon off and discard the layer of fat.

Tightly covered, the stock may safely be kept for three to four days in the refrigerator. Stored in small, well-covered freezer containers, the stock may be kept frozen for up to six months.

EDITOR'S NOTE: *The chicken gizzard and heart may be added to the stock, along with the bird's uncooked skin. Wings and necks — rich in natural gelatine — produce a particularly gelatinous stock, ideal for sauces and jellied dishes.*

Preparations for Colour and Flavour

The vibrant hues and piquant characters of aromatic vegetables and herbs give many hors-d'oeuvre their visual and gustatory appeal. The tomato is probably the most versatile and frequently used vegetable, adding both colour and bite to numerous dishes. For the best results choose firm-fleshed, preferably sun-ripened tomatoes; before cooking, skin, seed and chop them *(below)*. To release the fragrant oil of sweet peppers, roast or grill them and remove the peel *(opposite page, above)*.

Garlic, sliced, chopped or puréed — as here *(opposite page, below)* — adds spark to many dishes in this book. To peel a garlic clove, place the clove beneath the blade of a broad heavy knife and give the blade a thump to split the skin.

Many herbs — oregano, thyme, marjoram and savory, for example — are useful in a dried form, but most are at their best when fresh. They should be chopped with a clean sharp knife, just before using, and should have only minimal cooking. To keep herbs fresh for several days, simply roll them in a dampened cloth or paper towel and store them in the salad compartment of the refrigerator.

Chopping Parsley

1 *COARSE CHOPPING. Wash the parsley and pat it dry with a tea towel so that the leaves will not stick together. Grip the stems of the parsley, curling your fingertips back to protect them from the knife's blade, and slice through the leaves to cut them into thin shreds.*

2 *FINE CHOPPING. Gather the chopped parsley into a mound. Steady the tip of the knife with one hand while raising and lowering the knife handle with the other, moving the blade from side to side in an arc. Continue until the parsley is the desired size.*

Skinning and Seeding Tomatoes

1 *LOOSENING THE SKIN. With a small, sharp knife held at an angle, loosen a small column of flesh round the core at the stem end of the tomato and lift it out. Cut a small cross in the skin on the bottom of the tomato and plunge it into boiling water for 10 to 12 seconds.*

2 *PEELING. When the tomato is cool enough to handle, catch the skin between your thumb and the knife blade and strip it off in sections. Start at the cross cut in the base and work towards the stem end where the skin adheres more firmly.*

3 *SEEDING. Divide the tomato horizontally to expose the seed pockets. Gently squeeze a ripe tomato with your hand to force out the seeds. Alternatively, for a firm tomato, scrape out the seeds with a teaspoon (above), taking care not to damage the seed pockets.*

Peeling and Puréeing Peppers

1 PEELING THE PEPPERS. Roast whole peppers under a medium grill or in a hot oven, turning them occasionally, until their skins blister and blacken. Place them under a damp tea towel; the towel will trap the steam and loosen the skins. When the peppers are cool enough to handle, peel off the skins, working over a plate (above).

2 REMOVING THE SEEDS. Cut or tear open each pepper. Pull off the stem and the cluster of seeds attached to it. Use a teaspoon to pick out the remaining seeds. Discard the skin, stem and seeds, but reserve the pepper juices that have collected on the plate.

3 PURÉEING THE PEPPERS. Set a sturdy metal sieve over a bowl. Push the peppers through the sieve with a pestle. A pepper purée produced by sieving has more body and a more uniform consistency than one made by any other method. Add the pepper juice if desired, or reserve it for another purpose.

Puréeing Garlic

CRUSHING THE CLOVES. Place a few peeled garlic cloves in a mortar. Add about ¼ teaspoon of salt and pound together firmly with a pestle until the garlic is thoroughly pulverized with an almost liquid consistency.

1 *Cooked ahead of time to allow its flavours to mingle, this fragrant melange of vegetables contains only 3g of fat per serving (recipe, page 25).*

Cold Starters for All Seasons

A cold hors-d'oeuvre may be as simple as a mound of grated raw carrot lightly tossed in a lemony dressing *(page 16)*, or as elaborate as a multicoloured, layered terrine of salmon, sweet peppers and rice, which amply repays the time and effort spent on its preparation *(page 32)*. But whether they are destined to begin a family meal or launch a dinner party, the 50 dishes in this chapter have two things in common: all have been devised with a view to healthy eating, and most are easy to put together in advance, needing — at most — a few finishing touches at serving time.

The recipes that follow need not be treated as rigid formulae, but as starting points for experimentation with the best ingredients that the season has to offer. The large tossed salad on page 19, for instance, could be made with virtually any selection of fresh leaves and other raw or cooked ingredients. Success lies in knowing which of its elements will profit from marinating in vinaigrette dressing, and which should be added at the last minute. Cooked meat, poultry and fish, raw onions and most cooked vegetables (except for French beans and mange-tout) benefit from up to half an hour's steeping; salad leaves, fresh herbs and hard-boiled eggs are best incorporated at the moment the salad is tossed and served.

Throughout the chapter, familiar dishes appear in lighter guises. Sweet-and-sour herring, for example, is divested of its high-fat coating of soured cream and instead is bound with *fromage frais (page 45)*. Aubergines in tomato sauce, a Middle Eastern classic, usually consists of vegetables that have been sautéed in a large amount of oil; here the dish is rendered far more delicate, but equally delicious, by eliminating the frying stage *(page 30)*.

New ideas abound. Cold chicken, instead of being sauced as it so often is with cholesterol-laden mayonnaise, is dressed with a low-fat fruit vinaigrette *(page 54)*. Moulded cheese hearts, more commonly served as the rich dessert known as *coeurs à la crème*, appear on page 39 as a savoury hors-d'oeuvre based on a low-fat cheese mixture liberally seasoned with herbs and orange rind. Drawn from many different culinary traditions, yet reflecting a contemporary awareness of the need for a healthy, well-balanced diet, these and other recipes will expand any cook's repertoire of easily prepared first courses to fit all seasons, moods and menus.

Crudités

Raw vegetables, known by the French term crudités, make the simplest and healthiest of hors-d'oeuvre. They are free of fat and cholesterol, amply endowed with vitamins and minerals, and high in fibre.

Let the season and the market guide your choice. Small vegetables such as cherry tomatoes, button mushrooms, spring onions and young French beans can be left whole; others such as broccoli, cauliflower, carrots, cucumber, sweet pepper, chicory, cos lettuce, celery, fennel, kohlrabi and Chinese cabbage should be cut into manageable pieces. To serve, arrange the vegetables on a platter or in a basket, accompanied by oil and vinegar or one of the purées on the right.

For an equally quick and nutritious first course, raw or blanched vegetables may be sliced or grated and tossed in a light dressing (pages 16 and 17).

Haricot Bean Purée

GARLICKY PURÉES, LIBERALLY SEASONED WITH LEMON JUICE AND OLIVE OIL, ARE FOUND IN THE COOKERY OF VIRTUALLY ALL THE LANDS OF THE EASTERN MEDITERRANEAN. IN THIS RECIPE, THE ADDITION OF QUARK LIGHTENS THE PURÉE. THE QUARK'S HIGH PROTEIN CONTENT MAKES THIS PURÉE AN IDEAL FIRST COURSE FOR A VEGETARIAN MEAL.

Serves 16
Working time: about 45 minutes
Total time: about 15 hours
(includes soaking and chilling)

250 g	dried haricot beans, soaked overnight in enough water to cover them	8 oz
1	onion, quartered	1
4	large garlic cloves, peeled	4
2 tbsp	virgin olive oil	2 tbsp
2 tbsp	white wine vinegar	2 tbsp
½ tsp	salt	½ tsp
	freshly ground black pepper	
60 g	quark	2 oz
½ tsp	Dijon mustard	½ tsp
2 tbsp	fresh lemon juice	2 tbsp
1	sweet red pepper, skinned and seeded (page 11)	1
2 tbsp	finely chopped parsley	2 tbsp
1 tsp	chopped fresh rosemary, or ½ tsp dried rosemary	1 tsp

Calories **65**
Protein **4g**
Cholesterol **0mg**
Total fat **2g**
Saturated fat **0g**
Sodium **55mg**

Drain the beans in a colander and transfer them to a saucepan. Add the onion and garlic, cover the beans with cold water and bring them to the boil. Boil the beans vigorously for 15 minutes, then reduce the heat to low and simmer them until they are very tender — about 1½ hours. Drain the beans in a colander and let them cool for a few minutes.

Place the bean mixture, the oil and the vinegar in a food processor and blend the mixture to a purée. To give the purée a smooth texture, rub it through a fine sieve. Season with the salt and some pepper.

When the bean purée has cooled, mix in the quark, mustard and lemon juice. Dice the red pepper and fold it into the bean mixture with the parsley and rosemary. Turn the purée into a serving bowl and cover it. Refrigerate it for at least 4 hours to allow the flavours to blend. Remove the purée from the refrigerator about an hour before serving, to bring it up to room temperature.

SUGGESTED ACCOMPANIMENTS: *crudités (opposite); toast fingers or strips of warm pitta bread.*

Skordalia

SKORDALIA IS A RICH GREEK SAUCE CONTAINING GARLIC, OLIVE OIL AND BREAD, WITH A CONSISTENCY RESEMBLING THAT OF MAYONNAISE. IT IS TRADITIONALLY SERVED WITH RAW VEGETABLES, SEAFOOD OR HARD-BOILED EGGS. IN THIS LIGHTER VERSION, THE CREAMY TEXTURE IS RETAINED BUT THE FAT CONTENT IS REDUCED BY REPLACING SOME OF THE OLIVE OIL WITH *FROMAGE FRAIS*. NEVERTHELESS, A LITTLE GOES A LONG WAY.

Serves 18
Working (and total) time: about 15 minutes

5	cloves garlic, crushed	5
125 g	white bread, crusts removed	4 oz
2	parsley sprigs	2
2 tbsp	white wine vinegar	2 tbsp
½ tsp	salt	½ tsp
12.5 cl	virgin olive oil	4 fl oz
175 g	fromage frais	6 oz

Calories **90**
Protein **1g**
Cholesterol **0mg**
Total fat **8g**
Saturated fat **2g**
Sodium **80mg**

Place the garlic, bread and parsley sprigs in a food processor and blend until the mixture forms crumbs. Add the vinegar, salt and 3 tablespoons of water, and process until the mixture is thoroughly blended.

With the motor still running, begin adding the oil a teaspoon at a time, so that the sauce will not separate. When the sauce begins to thicken, pour in the rest of the oil in a thin stream, then add the *fromage frais*. Turn the skordalia into a shallow dish to serve.

SUGGESTED ACCOMPANIMENTS: *crudités (opposite); toast fingers or strips of warm pitta bread.*

Aubergine and Sesame Purée

Serves 14
Working time: about 20 minutes
Total time: about 5 hours (includes chilling)

2	aubergines (about 600g/1¼ lb)	2
1	large garlic clove, crushed	1
2 tbsp	virgin olive oil	2 tbsp
4 tbsp	fresh lemon juice	4 tbsp
2 tbsp	light tahini	2 tbsp
½ tsp	salt	½ tsp
	freshly ground black pepper	
3 tbsp	chopped fresh mint	3 tbsp

Calories **40**
Protein **1g**
Cholesterol **0mg**
Total fat **3g**
Saturated fat **1g**
Sodium **60mg**

Preheat the oven to 180°C (350°F or Mark 4). Prick the aubergines all over with a fork, place them on a baking sheet and bake them until they are soft and their skins are shrivelled — 45 minutes to 1 hour. Set them aside to cool.

When the aubergines are cool enough to handle, cut them in half lengthwise, scoop out the pulp, and transfer it to a food processor. Add the garlic and process the mixture to a fairly smooth purée.

Continue processing the purée while you pour in the oil, a little at a time. When all the oil has been incorporated, add the lemon juice, tahini, salt and some black pepper, and process the purée again until it is smooth and thoroughly blended. Turn the mixture into a bowl and fold in the chopped mint. Cover the bowl with plastic film and refrigerate the purée for at least 4 hours to allow its flavours to develop.

When you are ready to serve stir the mixture again and turn the chilled purée into a serving dish.

SUGGESTED ACCOMPANIMENTS: *crudités (opposite); toast fingers or strips of warm pitta bread.*

EDITOR'S NOTE: *If fresh mint is not available, flat-leaf parsley may be used instead.*

Celeriac in a Creamy Mustard Dressing

SIMPLE SALADS OF CELERIAC TOSSED IN A CREAMY
SAUCE APPEAR THROUGHOUT FRANCE AS STARTERS
FOR FAMILY MEALS AND ON RESTAURANT MENUS.

Serves 4
Working (and total) time: about 15 minutes

2 tsp	golden mustard seeds	2 tsp
½ tsp	Dijon mustard	½ tsp
½ tbsp	balsamic vinegar	½ tbsp
90 g	fromage frais	3 oz
1	celeriac (about 500 g/1 lb), peeled and cut into thin julienne	1

Calories **45**
Protein **3g**
Cholesterol **0mg**
Total fat **2g**
Saturated fat **1g**
Sodium **30mg**

In a small, heavy frying pan, heat the mustard seeds for a few seconds, until they begin to pop. Transfer the mustard seeds to a small bowl; mix in the Dijon mustard, balsamic vinegar and *fromage frais* to make a creamy dressing.

Place the celeriac strips in a serving bowl and toss them with the mustard dressing until they are thoroughly coated. Either serve the salad immediately or place it in the refrigerator until serving time, stirring it well just before you serve it.

Grated Carrot Salad

A SALAD OF GRATED RAW CARROTS MAKES A CRISP,
REFRESHING HORS-D'OEUVRE, RICH IN VITAMIN A. IT IS
PARTICULARLY WELCOME IN WINTER, WHEN MANY
FRESH SALAD INGREDIENTS ARE HARD TO COME BY.

Serves 4
Working (and total) time: about 10 minutes

60 g	fromage frais	2 oz
1 tbsp	fresh lemon juice	1 tbsp
½ tsp	grainy mustard	½ tsp
2 tsp	tarragon leaves, chopped	2 tsp
250 g	carrots, grated in a mouli julienne or in a food processor	8 oz

Calories **30**
Protein **2g**
Cholesterol **0mg**
Total fat **2g**
Saturated fat **1g**
Sodium **15mg**

In a small bowl, whisk together the *fromage frais*, lemon juice, mustard and tarragon leaves. Arrange the grated carrots in a large dish, spoon the dressing over them and serve the salad immediately.

French Beans with Anchovies and Lemon

Serves 4
Working (and total) time: about 25 minutes

250 g	French beans, topped and tailed	8 oz
3	anchovy fillets, soaked in a little milk for 15 minutes to reduce their saltiness	3
2 tbsp	virgin olive oil	2 tbsp
1 tbsp	fresh lemon juice	1 tbsp
½	lemon, roughly chopped, rind only	½
	freshly ground black pepper	
½	garlic clove	½
1 tbsp	finely cut chives	1 tbsp

Calories **95**
Protein **3g**
Cholesterol **0mg**
Total fat **8g**
Saturated fat **1g**
Sodium **100mg**

Fill a saucepan with water and parboil the French beans for 2 minutes. Drain the beans in a colander, refresh them under cold running water and drain them a second time. Remove the anchovies from the milk, drain them and pat them dry with kitchen paper. With a sharp knife, cut the fillets lengthwise into thin strips, then cut the strips horizontally to make 2.5 cm (1 inch) pieces.

To make the dressing, whisk together the oil and lemon juice in a small bowl. Stir in the lemon rind and some pepper. Rub a serving bowl with the garlic. Place the beans, anchovies, and chopped chives in the bowl and toss the beans with the dressing until they are well coated.

Tomatoes with Basil

A SIMPLE TOMATO SALAD MAKES A WONDERFUL HORS-D'OEUVRE IN HIGH SUMMER, WHEN FRESH TOMATOES ARE AT THEIR PEAK OF COLOUR AND FLAVOUR.

Serves 4
Working (and total) time: about 10 minutes

4	ripe tomatoes	4
6	basil leaves, cut into chiffonade	6
¼ tsp	salt	¼ tsp
1 tbsp	white wine vinegar	1 tbsp
2 tbsp	virgin olive oil	2 tbsp
	freshly ground black pepper	

Calories **80**
Protein **1g**
Cholesterol **0mg**
Total fat **8g**
Saturated fat **1g**
Sodium **100mg**

With a sharp knife, cut the four tomatoes into thin slices. Arrange the slices on a serving plate, slightly overlapping, and sprinkle the shredded basil leaves over them.

In a small bowl, stir the salt and vinegar together until the salt dissolves. Whisk in the olive oil, beating until the oil and vinegar are thoroughly blended. Dress the tomato slices with the vinaigrette, add plenty of black pepper and serve the salad immediately.

Baby Courgettes Vinaigrette

Serves 4
Working (and total) time: about 15 minutes

500 g	baby courgettes	1 lb
1	garlic clove, finely chopped	1
¼ tsp	salt	¼ tsp
1 tsp	grainy mustard	1 tsp
½ tsp	Dijon mustard	½ tsp
	freshly ground black pepper	
1 tbsp	white wine vinegar	1 tbsp
2 tbsp	virgin olive oil	2 tbsp
7	purple basil leaves, torn	7

Calories **90**
Protein **1g**
Cholesterol **0mg**
Total fat **8g**
Saturated fat **1g**
Sodium **200mg**

With a sharp knife, slice the courgettes diagonally into 2.5 cm (1 inch) pieces and plunge them into a saucepan filled with boiling water. Boil the courgettes until they are just tender — about 5 minutes.

While the courgettes cook, prepare the dressing. Place the garlic and the salt in a mortar and pound them with a pestle until the garlic has broken down into a purée. Mix in the two mustards, the pepper and the vinegar, then whisk in the olive oil.

Remove the courgettes from the heat, drain them in a colander, and refresh them quickly under cold running water to arrest their cooking. Drain them thoroughly again.

Transfer the drained courgettes on to a shallow serving dish. Toss them with the mustard dressing and the basil leaves, and serve the salad immediately.

EDITOR'S NOTE: *If purple basil is unavailable, use ordinary fresh basil leaves instead.*

Fennel Salad

Serves 4
Working (and total) time: about 10 minutes

½ tsp	salt	½ tsp
1 tbsp	white wine vinegar	1 tbsp
2 tbsp	virgin olive oil	2 tbsp
3 tbsp	finely chopped parsley	3 tbsp
	white pepper	
2	fennel bulbs, sliced	2

Calories **75**
Protein **1g**
Cholesterol **0mg**
Total fat **8g**
Saturated fat **1g**
Sodium **265mg**

In a small bowl, stir the salt and vinegar together until the salt dissolves. Add the olive oil, parsley and some white pepper, whisking until the dressing is well blended.

Place the fennel slices in a serving bowl. Toss them with the vinaigrette dressing just before serving.

Salad of Leaves and Flowers

EDIBLE FLOWERS, SUCH AS VIOLETS, ROSE PETALS AND NASTURTIUM LEAVES, ADD COLOUR AND PIQUANCY TO SIMPLE TOSSED SALADS. SOME GREENGROCERS AND SUPERMARKETS NOW STOCK A VARIETY OF EDIBLE BLOOMS. IF YOU ARE USING GARDEN FLOWERS, AVOID ANY THAT HAVE BEEN SPRAYED WITH CHEMICALS AND INSECTICIDES. FLOWERS SOLD BY FLORISTS SHOULD NOT BE USED FOR CULINARY PURPOSES.

Serves 6
Working (and total) time: about 10 minutes

Calories **75**
Protein **1g**
Cholesterol **0mg**
Total fat **8g**
Saturated fat **1g**
Sodium **5mg**

1	lettuce heart, separated into leaves, washed and dried	1
5	oak leaf lettuce leaves, washed and dried	5
30 g	curly endive, washed and dried	1 oz
8	nasturtium leaves	8
2 tsp	lavender florets	2 tsp
1 tsp	borage flowers	1 tsp
2 tsp	thyme flowers	2 tsp
8	rose petals	8
6	violets or pansies	6
6	chervil sprigs	6
Tarragon vinaigrette		
3 tbsp	safflower oil	3 tbsp
1 ½ tbsp	white wine vinegar	1 ½ tbsp
1 tsp	crushed coriander seeds	1 tsp
	freshly ground black pepper	
½ tsp	fresh tarragon leaves	½ tsp

In a small bowl, whisk together the oil and the vinegar for the dressing. Stir in the coriander seeds, some pepper and the tarragon, and mix well.

Lay the lettuce, the endive and the nasturtium leaves loosely in a deep bowl. Sprinkle the lavender, borage and thyme flowers, the rose petals, the violets or pansies and the chervil over the top. Add the dressing, toss the salad and serve it immediately.

EDITOR'S NOTE: *Any selection of mild and bitter salad leaves and edible flowers can be used. Aim for a combination that offers vivid contrasts of colour, flavour and texture. Perfect freshness of all ingredients is the sole requirement.*

Tossed Salad with Eggs and French Beans

Serves 6
Working time: about 15 minutes
Total time: about 40 minutes (includes marinating)

Calories **115**
Protein **3g**
Cholesterol **75mg**
Total fat **10g**
Saturated fat **2g**
Sodium **100mg**

½	small red onion, cut thinly into rings	½
1	small red lollo lettuce, washed and dried, leaves torn	1
30 g	rocket, washed and dried	1 oz
90 g	French beans, topped and blanched for 3 minutes in boiling water	3 oz
2	eggs, hard-boiled, each cut into six wedges	2
6	black olives	6
3	red basil sprigs	3
3	green basil sprigs	3
Vinaigrette dressing		
1	garlic clove, crushed	1
¼ tsp	salt	¼ tsp
	freshly ground black pepper	
1 tbsp	red wine vinegar	1 tbsp
3 tbsp	virgin olive oil	3 tbsp

First prepare the vinaigrette. Place the garlic, salt and some pepper in a large salad bowl. Using a wooden pestle, pound the ingredients until they break down into a paste. Add the vinegar and stir until the salt dissolves. Pour in the olive oil and mix thoroughly.

With your hands or the pestle, stir the onion slices into the vinaigrette to coat them well. Set them aside to marinate for 30 minutes.

Cross a pair of salad servers over the bottom of the bowl, to keep the dressing separate from the leaves that will be added before the salad is tossed. Lay a few of the largest lettuce leaves on the servers, then fill the bowl with the remaining lettuce and the rocket.

Top the leaves with the French beans, hard-boiled eggs, olives and basil. Draw out the servers from the bed of lettuce and rocket and toss the salad with the servers, or by hand, until all its ingredients are lightly coated with the dressing.

Artichoke and Potato Bowl

Serves 4
Working time: about 20 minutes
Total time: about 1 hour and 20 minutes (includes chilling)

Calories **150**
Protein **2 g**
Cholesterol **0 mg**
Total fat **10 g**
Saturated fat **2 g**
Sodium **35 mg**

2 tbsp	fresh lemon juice or vinegar	2 tbsp
350 g	baby artichokes, stems cut off flush with base, tough outer leaves removed and discarded (page 26, Step 1)	12 oz
250 g	small new potatoes, scrubbed	8 oz
1	small head radicchio, washed and dried	1
1	small head lettuce, washed and dried	1
2 tbsp	finely cut chives	2 tbsp
Balsamic vinaigrette		
1 tbsp	balsamic vinegar	1 tbsp
¼ tsp	dry mustard	¼ tsp
½	garlic clove, finely chopped	½
	freshly ground black pepper	
2½ tbsp	virgin olive oil	2½ tbsp

Add the lemon juice or vinegar to a large saucepan of boiling water and drop in the artichokes. Submerge the artichokes by weighting them down with a heavy plate or the lid from a smaller saucepan, and cook them until tender — 20 to 25 minutes. Drain the artichokes in a colander and set them aside to cool. Meanwhile, cut

the potatoes in half and cook them in a covered pan of boiling water until tender — about 12 minutes.

To make the vinaigrette, place the balsamic vinegar in a small jar with a lid and add the mustard, garlic and some pepper. Shake or stir the ingredients to combine them, then add the oil. Cover the jar and shake it to mix everything well.

When the potatoes are cooked, transfer them to a large bowl. Shake the jar of dressing again and add some of the dressing while the potatoes are hot. Toss the potatoes to coat them well.

Cut off the top 2.5 cm (1 inch) of the cooked artichokes and gently remove any outer leaves that are still fibrous. Cut the artichokes in half lengthwise and remove the fuzzy choke if there is one. Add the artichoke halves to the potatoes. Shake the jar of dressing again and add the remaining dressing to the salad. Toss the vegetables carefully to combine them. Cover the salad with plastic film and chill it in the refrigerator for about 30 minutes.

Line a large salad bowl with the radicchio and lettuce, scatter the salad over the lettuces and sprinkle it with chopped chives before serving.

EDITOR'S NOTE: *The dressing for the salad may also be made with a good quality wine vinegar, although the resulting vinaigrette will be less aromatic than with balsamic vinegar.*

Caesar Salad

PREREQUISITES FOR THE CLASSIC CAESAR SALAD INCLUDE DEEP-FRIED CROÛTONS AND A RAW EGG IN THE DRESSING. IN THIS LIGHTER VERSION THE FRIED CROÛTONS ARE REPLACED BY CUBES OF TOASTED WHOLEMEAL BREAD.

Serves 4
Working (and total) time: about 30 minutes

Calories **120**
Protein **6g**
Cholesterol **35mg**
Total fat **8g**
Saturated fat **2g**
Sodium **400mg**

30 g	radicchio, washed and dried	1 oz
90 g	Batavian endive, washed and dried	3 oz
90 g	cos lettuce, washed and dried	3 oz
2	thin slices wholemeal bread	2
30 g	anchovy fillets	1 oz
15 g	freshly grated Parmesan cheese	½ oz
Egg and lemon dressing		
½	beaten small egg	½
1 tbsp	virgin olive oil	1 tbsp
1 tbsp	fresh lemon juice	1 tbsp
1 tbsp	finely grated lemon rind	1 tbsp
1	small garlic clove, crushed	1

Tear the salad leaves and put them into a large salad bowl. Cover the bowl with plastic film and place in the refrigerator for 20 to 30 minutes to crisp the leaves.

Meanwhile, toast the slices of wholemeal bread until they are golden-brown. Remove the crusts and cut the toast into small dice. Drain the anchovy fillets thoroughly on absorbent kitchen paper, then chop them roughly.

Just before serving, put the dressing ingredients into a bowl and whisk them until they are thoroughly blended. Remove the salad leaves from the refrigerator, and sprinkle them with the diced toast, chopped anchovy fillets and grated Parmesan cheese. Pour the dressing over the salad, toss it gently and serve immediately.

Spinach Roulade

Serves 6
Working time: about 1 hour
Total time: about 2 hours (includes cooling)

Calories **165**
Protein **10g**
Cholesterol **75mg**
Total fat **8g**
Saturated fat **2g**
Sodium **280mg**

350 g	fresh spinach, stemmed, washed but not dried	12 oz
45 g	plain flour	1½ oz
30 cl	skimmed milk	½ pint
½ tsp	dry mustard	½ tsp
1 tsp	salt	1 tsp
	freshly ground black pepper	
2	egg yolks	2
4	egg whites	4
1 tbsp	fresh Parmesan cheese, finely grated	1 tbsp
Mushroom and pepper filling		
125 g	chestnut or button mushrooms, finely diced	4 oz
½	sweet red pepper, cored, seeded and finely diced	½
½	sweet yellow pepper, cored, seeded and finely diced	½
3	spring onions, thinly sliced	3
1 tbsp	virgin olive oil	1 tbsp
100 g	fromage frais	3½ oz

Put the spinach in a large saucepan, cover the pan and cook the spinach over high heat in the water clinging to its leaves until it begins to wilt. Remove the lid and continue cooking the spinach over medium heat, turning frequently, until the spinach has wilted completely — 5 to 7 minutes. Drain the spinach in a colander, pressing out all excess water with a saucer or a wooden spoon. Transfer the spinach to a food processor, blend it to a smooth purée, and set it aside. Preheat the oven to 170°C (325°F or Mark 3).

In a bowl, mix the flour to a paste with a little of the milk. Put the remaining milk in a small saucepan and heat it until bubbles appear round the edge. Add the hot milk to the flour paste and whisk until the sauce is perfectly smooth. (If any lumps of flour remain, rub the mixture through a fine sieve.) Pour the sauce into the saucepan and cook it over medium heat, stirring briskly, until it thickens and comes to the boil. Reduce the heat and simmer the sauce for 5 minutes, stirring constantly.

Cool the sauce slightly, then add it to the spinach purée in the food processor, along with the mustard, the salt and some pepper. Blend the ingredients thoroughly. Add the egg yolks and blend again briefly. Turn the mixture into a bowl.

In another bowl, beat the egg whites until they are stiff. Fold the beaten whites into the spinach sauce with a metal spoon. Line a 30 by 20 cm (12 by 8 inch) Swiss roll tin with greaseproof paper and oil the paper. Spread out the spinach mixture evenly in the tin and bake it until it is risen and just set — 35 to 40 minutes.

While it bakes, prepare the filling. Heat the oil in a non-stick frying pan. Cook the mushrooms, red and yellow peppers and spring onions over medium heat, stirring frequently, until they are tender but still firm — 4 to 5 minutes. Remove the vegetables from the heat, transfer them to a colander to drain off their liquid, and leave them to cool.

Place a sheet of greaseproof paper, slightly larger than the Swiss roll tin, on a flat surface and sprinkle it evenly with the grated Parmesan cheese. When the spinach roulade mixture is cooked, turn it out on to the cheese-coated paper. Peel off the lining paper very carefully and trim away any crusty edges from the spinach base. Then roll up the spinach base together with the cheese-coated paper, and set the roll aside to cool.

When the vegetables are cold, mix them with the *fromage frais*. Unroll the spinach base, remove the paper and spread the filling over the spinach. Roll up the roulade again, and place it seam side down on a serving dish.

Cut the roulade into slices and serve immediately.

Aubergines in Tomato Sauce

THIS IS A VARIATION ON THE CLASSIC TURKISH DISH *IMAM BAYILDI*,
WHICH TRANSLATES LITERALLY AS "THE HOLY MAN FAINTED".
TRADITIONALLY, THE AUBERGINE IS FRIED IN A LARGE AMOUNT OF
OIL; HERE IT IS SIMMERED IN A TOMATO SAUCE.

Serves 6
Working time: about 20 minutes
Total time: about 2 hours

Calories **100**
Protein **3g**
Cholesterol **0mg**
Total fat **6g**
Saturated fat **1g**
Sodium **75mg**

500 g	aubergines, sliced	1 lb
1¼ tsp	salt	1¼ tsp
2 tbsp	virgin olive oil	2 tbsp
1	onion, sliced	1
2	garlic cloves, chopped	2
750 g	ripe tomatoes, skinned, seeded (page 10) and chopped, or 400 g (14 oz) canned tomatoes, drained and coarsely chopped	1½ lb
1 tsp	tomato paste	1 tsp
1	bay leaf	1
	freshly ground black pepper	
15 g	pine-nuts, tossed in a heavy frying pan over medium heat until golden-brown	½ oz
1 tbsp	chopped parsley	1 tbsp

Sprinkle the aubergine slices with 1 teaspoon of the salt and let them drain in a colander for 30 minutes to draw out their bitter juices. Meanwhile, heat the oil in a large, heavy-bottomed saucepan, and fry the sliced onion and the garlic until they are softened. Add the chopped tomatoes, tomato paste, bay leaf, the remaining salt and some pepper, then cover the pan and simmer the sauce for 10 minutes.

Rinse the aubergines in cold water and pat them dry with kitchen paper. Add the aubergines to the pan,

Lay any spare or damaged vine leaves in the base of a heavy casserole. Set the stuffed parcels in the casserole, packing them in tightly to keep them from unrolling. Pour the oil, lemon juice and 45 cl (¾ pint) of water over the rolls.

Cover the casserole and cook the vine leaves in the oven for about 1¼ hours, adding extra water if the liquid in the casserole evaporates. Leave the parcels to cool in the casserole. Serve them cold, garnished with lemon wedges.

EDITOR'S NOTE: *Preserved vine leaves may be used if fresh leaves are not available. Wash them in cold water to rid them of excess salt, then drain them thoroughly on a folded tea towel. They do not require blanching.*

Chicken-Stuffed Peppers

Serves 6
Working time: about 45 minutes
Total time: about 7 hours (includes chilling)

Calories **140**
Protein **9g**
Cholesterol **20mg**
Total fat **4g**
Saturated fat **1g**
Sodium **75mg**

3	small sweet red peppers, tops cut off and reserved, seeds and ribs removed	3
3	small sweet yellow peppers, tops cut off and reserved, seeds and ribs removed	3
15 cl	unsalted chicken stock (recipe, page 9)	¼ pint
1 tbsp	virgin olive oil	1 tbsp
Spiced chicken stuffing		
½ tbsp	virgin olive oil	½ tbsp
1	onion, finely chopped	1
125 g	long-grain rice	4 oz
2	garlic cloves, crushed	2
½ tsp	ground cardamom	½ tsp
½ tsp	ground cumin	½ tsp
250 g	boned chicken breast, skinned and cut into tiny cubes	8 oz
30 cl	unsalted chicken stock (recipe, page 9)	½ pint
¼ tsp	salt	¼ tsp
	freshly ground black pepper	

First prepare the stuffing. In a large saucepan, heat the oil, then add the onion and cook gently until the onion has softened but not browned — 5 to 6 minutes. Stir in the rice, garlic, cardamom and cumin. Cook for 1 to 2 minutes, then stir in the chicken pieces, stock, salt and some pepper. Bring the mixture to the boil, reduce the heat, cover the pan with a tightly fitting lid and cook very gently until the rice is tender and all of the stock has been absorbed — 25 to 30 minutes.

Preheat the oven to 180°C (350°F or Mark 4).

Cook the peppers and their lids in boiling water until they soften slightly — 4 to 5 minutes. Place the peppers in a large colander, refresh them under cold running water and drain them well.

Fill the peppers with the rice and chicken mixture and cover them with their lids. Stand the peppers in a deep ovenproof dish, add the chicken stock and cover the dish with a lid or with foil. Bake the peppers in the oven until they are very tender — about 1½ hours.

Using a slotted spoon, carefully transfer the cooked peppers to a serving dish. Pour the juices left in the baking dish into a saucepan, bring them to the boil and boil rapidly until they are reduced by half, then whisk in the olive oil. Pour this liquid over the peppers, and set them aside to cool. When the peppers have cooled, cover them with plastic film and place them in the refrigerator until they are well chilled — 3 to 4 hours, or overnight — before serving.

Melon, Bacon and Mint Melange

Serves 4
Working (and total) time: about 20 minutes

Calories **130**
Protein **5g**
Cholesterol **15mg**
Total fat **10g**
Saturated fat **3g**
Sodium **290mg**

½	Gallia or other green melon	½
1	small cantaloupe or Charentais melon	1
125 g	cucumber	4 oz
2	lean rashers bacon (about 60 g/2 oz)	2
2 tbsp	fresh lemon juice	2 tbsp
1 tbsp	safflower oil	1 tbsp
	freshly ground black pepper	
40	young mint leaves	40

Peel the melons with a sharp knife Discard their seeds, and cut the flesh into 2.5 cm (1 inch) cubes. Using a vegetable peeler, remove thin strips of peel lengthwise from the cucumber to produce a striped effect. Slice the cucumber into paper-thin rounds.

Cut off and discard the bacon rind and fat, then cook the rashers in a heavy, ungreased frying pan until they are crisp. Remove the bacon from the pan and lay it on paper towels to drain.

Cut the bacon into short strips and place them in a mixing bowl with the melon cubes and cucumber slices. Toss the bacon and fruit gently together, and transfer the salad to individual serving plates.

Add the lemon juice and oil to the frying pan and cook the mixture for a few minutes over gentle heat, stirring and scraping loose the meaty residues on the bottom of the pan.

Stir the mint leaves into the hot lemon juice and oil mixture and spoon the dressing over the salad. Serve the salad immediately.

Summer Fruits with Hazelnut Dressing

A SAVOURY FRUIT SALAD MAKES A REFRESHING OPENING TO A
HOT-WEATHER MEAL, ESPECIALLY IF THE SERVING PLATES ARE
CHILLED FOR AN HOUR IN ADVANCE.

Serves 6
Working time: about 15 minutes
Total time: about 1 hour

Calories **145**
Protein **2g**
Cholesterol **0mg**
Total fat **7g**
Saturated fat **1g**
Sodium **10mg**

4	ripe peaches, peeled and sliced	4
1 tbsp	fresh lemon juice	1 tbsp
1	mango, peeled and sliced	1
250 g	blueberries	8 oz
250 g	strawberries, halved	8 oz
2 tbsp	hazelnut oil	2 tbsp
6	basil leaves	6

Place six serving plates in the refrigerator until well chilled — about 1 hour. Rub the peach slices with a little of the lemon juice to prevent discoloration. Arrange the peaches, mango slices, blueberries and strawberry halves on the chilled serving plates.

In a small jug, stir the hazelnut oil and the remaining lemon juice with a fork until thoroughly blended, and dribble this dressing over the fruit. Garnish each plate with a basil leaf, and serve the salad immediately.

EDITOR'S NOTE: *Perfectly ripe persimmons (also known as sharon fruit) can be used instead of peaches.*

Figs with Goat Cheese
and Walnuts

Serves 8
Working (and total) time: about 30 minutes

Calories **135**
Protein **6g**
Cholesterol **20mg**
Total fat **10g**
Saturated fat **4g**
Sodium **75mg**

8	ripe green or purple figs	8
8	walnuts, shelled and chopped	8
175 g	soft goat cheese	6 oz
Herb dressing		
2 tbsp	walnut or virgin olive oil	2 tbsp
2 tbsp	white wine vinegar	2 tbsp
4 tsp	finely chopped parsley	4 tsp
2 tsp	finely chopped fresh thyme	2 tsp
½ tsp	salt	½ tsp
	freshly ground black pepper	

With a sharp knife, slice the tops off the figs and reserve them to be used as lids for the stuffed fruit. Hollow out the figs with a small spoon, transfer their pulp to a bowl, and mix it with the chopped walnuts. Set the mixture aside.

In a small bowl, mix together the oil and the white wine vinegar with a fork until thoroughly blended. Add the parsley, thyme, salt and some freshly ground black pepper to complete the dressing.

With the back of a fork, blend the goat cheese with the fig and walnut mixture, and spoon this filling into the figs, packing the mixture down into the hollows. Spoon the dressing over the stuffed fruit, replace the reserved tops on the figs, and serve.

Savoury Cheese Hearts

THIS IS A LOW-FAT VARIATION OF THE RICH CREAM AND CHEESE
MOULDS THAT IN FRENCH CUISINE ARE CALLED
COEURS À LA CRÈME.

Serves 4
Working time: about 15 minutes
Total time: about 12 hours (includes draining)

Calories **100**
Protein **7g**
Cholesterol **0mg**
Total fat **7g**
Saturated fat **4g**
Sodium **210mg**

350 g	fromage frais	12 oz
1 tsp	finely chopped fresh mint	1 tsp
1 tsp	finely chopped fresh lemon verbena or parsley	1 tsp
1 tsp	finely chopped fresh basil	1 tsp
1 tsp	finely grated orange rind	1 tsp
½ tsp	whole coriander seeds	½ tsp
¼ tsp	salt	¼ tsp
1	large egg white	1
	fresh herbs, such as mint, parsley and basil, for garnish	
	thin strips of orange rind for garnish	

Beat the soft cheese lightly, and combine it with the chopped mint, lemon verbena or parsley, basil, orange rind, coriander seeds and salt. In a clean, dry bowl, whisk the egg white until it is fairly stiff, then fold it gently but thoroughly into the cheese mixture.

Line four perforated heart-shaped moulds with dampened squares of muslin, smoothing out wrinkles. Gently fill each mould with the cheese mixture, set the moulds over a tray or deep platter, and leave to drain for about 12 hours, or overnight, in a cool place.

Invert the hearts on to individual serving dishes and garnish them with fresh herbs and orange rind.

EDITOR'S NOTE: *These cheese hearts are very delicate. If they break or are damaged while being unmoulded, you can repair them by dipping a rounded knife or palette knife in water and using it to pat the cheese mixture back into shape.*

Salmon Tartare

THIS RECIPE IS INSPIRED BY THE CLASSIC HORS-D'OEUVRE OF
HIGHLY SEASONED RAW BEEF KNOWN AS STEAK TARTARE.

Serves 4
Working time: about 20 minutes
Total time: about 1 hour and 20 minutes (includes chilling)

Calories **200**
Protein **12g**
Cholesterol **55mg**
Total fat **12g**
Saturated fat **5g**
Sodium **195mg**

250 g	salmon fillet, skinned and finely chopped	8 oz
½ tsp	freshly ground black pepper	½ tsp
2	spring onions, finely sliced	2
1	lime, finely grated rind only	1
6 tbsp	soured cream	6 tbsp
4	thin slices wholemeal bread, toasted, crusts removed, cut into triangles	4

In a bowl, mix the chopped fish thoroughly with the black pepper and combine it with the spring onions. Chill the salmon mixture in the refrigerator for 1 hour.

In the meantime, stir most of the grated lime rind into the soured cream. Place the soured cream mixture and four individual serving plates in the refrigerator to chill with the salmon.

At serving time, divide the salmon tartare among the four chilled plates, forming each portion into a small mound with a hollow in its centre. Spoon a quarter of the soured cream mixture into each hollow and sprinkle on the remaining lime rind. Serve the fish accompanied by the wholemeal toast.

EDITOR'S NOTE: *Because the salmon in this recipe is not cooked, only the freshest fish should be used.*

Pickled Peppers with Mussels

Serves 4
Working time: about 25 minutes
Total time: about 1 hour and 15 minutes (includes chilling)

Calories **100**
Protein **14g**
Cholesterol **10mg**
Total fat **2g**
Saturated fat **0g**
Sodium **150mg**

1	sweet red pepper, seeded, deribbed and thinly sliced	1
1	sweet green pepper, seeded, deribbed and thinly sliced	1
1	sweet yellow pepper, seeded, deribbed and thinly sliced	1
2	garlic cloves, peeled and thinly sliced	2
6 tbsp	white wine vinegar	6 tbsp
1 tbsp	demerara sugar	1 tbsp
2 tbsp	chopped parsley	2 tbsp
20	large mussels (about 500 g/1 lb), scrubbed and debearded	20

Place the sliced sweet peppers in a medium-sized saucepan with the garlic, wine vinegar and sugar. Bring the vinegar to the boil, then cover the pan and reduce the heat; simmer the peppers for 7 minutes. Stir in 1 tablespoon of the chopped parsley, and allow the peppers and their liquor to cool.

Put 3 tablespoons of water and the mussels in a large saucepan, cover the pan and bring the water to the boil. Steam the mussels until they open — 3 to 4 minutes. Drain the mussels in a colander, discarding the liquid and any mussels that remain closed. Leave the mussels to cool.

Chill the peppers and the mussels in the refrigerator for at least 30 minutes before serving. To serve, divide the peppers among four individual plates, arrange the mussels on the peppers, pour over the pepper liquor and sprinkle the remaining parsley on top.

SUGGESTED ACCOMPANIMENT: *crusty bread.*

Marinated Sardines

ONLY THE FRESHEST FISH SHOULD BE USED FOR THIS TRADITIONAL SPANISH HORS-D'OEUVRE. THE SARDINE FILLETS ARE MARINATED FOR TWO TO THREE DAYS IN AN OIL AND VINEGAR MIXTURE, WHICH TENDERIZES THE FLESH, AND THE FISH IS SERVED UNCOOKED.

Serves 6
Working time: about 45 minutes
Total time: 2 to 3 days (includes marinating)

Calories **110**
Protein **9g**
Cholesterol **40mg**
Total fat **8g**
Saturated fat **2g**
Sodium **105mg**

600 g	fresh sardines, scaled, heads and tails removed, gutted, rinsed and patted dry	1¼ lb
¾ tsp	salt	¾ tsp
2	garlic cloves, chopped	2
1 tbsp	chopped parsley	1 tbsp
1 tbsp	virgin olive oil	1 tbsp
12.5 cl	wine vinegar	4 fl oz

Remove the backbone from each sardine and separate the two fillets lengthwise, leaving the skin intact.

Sprinkle the fish with the salt and place a layer of the fillets, skin side uppermost, in a shallow, non-reactive dish. Top the sardines with the garlic and parsley. If the dish is not large enough to accommodate all the sardines in a single layer, add a second layer on top of the first.

Pour the oil and the vinegar over the fish, until the mixture covers the sardines. Cover the dish with plastic film and place it in the refrigerator to marinate for two to three days before serving.

SUGGESTED ACCOMPANIMENT: *crusty bread.*

EDITOR'S NOTE: *Fresh anchovies or small sprats, no longer than 12 cm (5 inches), can be used instead of sardines.*

Rainbow Trout with Yogurt Dressing

THIS PROTEIN-RICH SALAD MAKES A SUBSTANTIAL STARTER TO PRECEDE A LIGHT, MEATLESS MAIN COURSE SUCH AS PASTA OR A VEGETABLE STEW.

Serves 6
Working time: about 20 minutes
Total time: about 30 minutes

Calories **165**
Protein **18g**
Cholesterol **35mg**
Total fat **9g**
Saturated fat **2g**
Sodium **155mg**

3	rainbow trout (about 750 g/1 ½ lb), cleaned	3
4 tbsp	white wine	4 tbsp
250 g	mixed washed and dried salad leaves, herbs and edible flowers, such as rocket, curly endive, oakleaf lettuce, chervil and borage flowers	8 oz
17.5 cl	plain low-fat yogurt	6 fl oz
½	lemon, juice only	½
2 tsp	finely chopped fresh dill	2 tsp
2 tbsp	virgin olive oil	2 tbsp
⅛ tsp	salt	⅛ tsp
	freshly ground black pepper	

Preheat the oven to 200°C (400°F or Mark 6). Place the three trout on a rectangle of foil measuring approximately 35 by 30 cm (14 by 12 inches). Sprinkle the white wine over the fish, wrap them securely in the foil, and bake them in the oven for 15 minutes. Remove the trout from the foil and set them aside to cool.

Arrange the salad leaves and flowers on a large platter or on individual serving plates. To prepare the dressing, mix the yogurt, lemon juice, dill, oil, salt and some pepper in a small bowl.

When the fish is cool enough to handle, skin and fillet it, and break the flesh into bite-sized pieces.

Just before serving, dribble the yogurt dressing over the leaves and flowers and arrange the trout pieces on top of the salad.

EDITOR'S NOTE: For the use of flowers in salads, see page 18.

Barquettes with Three Fillings

Serves 6
Working time: about 1 hour
Total time: about 2 hours and 15 minutes (includes chilling)

Calories **260**
Protein **12g**
Cholesterol **40mg**
Total fat **15g**
Saturated fat **4g**
Sodium **490mg**

125 g	plain flour	4 oz
1/8 tsp	salt	1/8 tsp
60 g	polyunsaturated margarine	2 oz
1/2	beaten egg	1/2
Smoked mackerel mousse		
175 g	smoked mackerel fillet, skinned and any bones removed	6 oz
15 g	polyunsaturated margarine	1/2 oz
1/4 tsp	salt	1/4 tsp
	freshly ground black pepper	
2 tsp	fresh lemon juice	2 tsp
3	thin slices of lemon, cut into quarters	3
Asparagus cream		
175 g	thin asparagus spears, trimmed	6 oz
1 tbsp	soured cream	1 tbsp
1/8 tsp	salt	1/8 tsp
	freshly ground black pepper	
Prawn salad		
1 tsp	virgin olive oil	1 tsp
1 tsp	wine vinegar	1 tsp
1	garlic clove, crushed	1
2 tsp	finely chopped parsley	2 tsp
	freshly ground black pepper	
90 g	peeled prawns	3 oz
2	lettuce leaves, washed, dried and shredded	2

To make the pastry, sift the flour and salt into a mixing bowl. Rub the margarine into the flour until the mixture resembles fine breadcrumbs. Mix the dry ingredients together with the beaten egg and 1 to 2 tablespoons of cold water to make a firm dough.

On a floured surface, roll the dough out very thinly. Cut it into strips long and wide enough to line eighteen 9.5 cm (3¾ inch) long barquette tins. (If you do not have that many tins, bake the pastry cases in batches.) Prick the dough all over with a fork, then place the tins on a baking sheet and refrigerate for 30 minutes. Preheat the oven to 220°C (425°F or Mark 7).

Bake the pastry cases until they are very lightly browned — 10 to 15 minutes. Carefully remove the pastry cases from the tins and transfer them to a wire rack to cool while you prepare the three fillings.

To make the smoked mackerel mousse, flake the fish and put it into a food processor or blender with the margarine, salt, some pepper and the lemon juice. Blend until the mixture is smooth and creamy. Spoon the filling into a small bowl, cover it with plastic film and place it in the refrigerator to chill.

To make the asparagus cream, boil the asparagus in 2.5 cm (1 inch) of water in a frying pan, until tender — about 3 minutes. Drain the spears and refresh them under cold running water. When cool, remove the tips from six of the spears and set them aside to use as a garnish. Finely chop the remaining asparagus and put it in a small bowl. Add the soured cream, salt and some pepper, and mix well. Cover the filling with plastic film and place it in the refrigerator.

To make the prawn salad, put the oil, vinegar, garlic and parsley into a small bowl, season with pepper and stir well. Mix the prawns with this dressing, cover with plastic film and refrigerate with the two other fillings. Chill all three fillings for at least 1 hour.

To complete the barquettes, remove the fillings from the refrigerator about 20 to 30 minutes before serving. Spoon the smoked mackerel mousse into six boats and garnish with the lemon pieces. Fill another six boats with the asparagus cream and top with the reserved asparagus tips. Fill the remaining boats with a little shredded lettuce, topped with the prawns.

Sole and Asparagus Tartlets

Serves 6
Working time: about 1 hour
Total time: about 3 hours (includes chilling)

Calories **240**
Protein **12g**
Cholesterol **50mg**
Total fat **13g**
Saturated fat **3g**
Sodium **260mg**

175 g	skinned sole fillets	6 oz
1	egg white	1
150 g	plus 2 tbsp thick Greek yogurt	5 oz
¼ tsp	salt	¼ tsp
	freshly ground black pepper	
250 g	asparagus, trimmed, peeled and thinly sliced	8 oz
45 g	smoked salmon, cut into fine strips	1½ oz
2 tsp	finely cut chives	2 tsp
	thinly sliced cucumber, for garnish	
Tartlet shells		
125 g	plain flour	4 oz
⅛ tsp	salt	⅛ tsp
60 g	polyunsaturated margarine	2 oz
1	egg yolk	1

To prepare the filling, place the sole fillets and egg white in a food processor and process them until they form a smooth paste. Set a nylon sieve over a bowl, and work the paste through the sieve to remove any coarse fibres. Cover the bowl with plastic film and refrigerate the sole and egg mixture while you prepare the tartlet shells.

To make the pastry, sift the flour and salt into a mixing bowl. Rub the margarine into the flour until the mixture resembles fine breadcrumbs; make a well in the centre. Pour the egg yolk and 1 tablespoon of water into the well and mix the ingredients, using a table knife or your hands, until a firm dough is formed.

Knead the dough on a lightly floured surface, then roll the dough out thinly. Cut out six rounds of dough measuring about 12.5 cm (5 inches) in diameter. Line six 10 cm (4 inch) fluted tartlet tins with the dough, pressing it well into the flutes and trimming the edges. Prick the pastry lightly with a fork, and refrigerate it for 30 minutes. Meanwhile, preheat the oven to 220°C (425°F or Mark 7).

Remove the chilled sole from the refrigerator. Gradually beat in 12.5 cl (4 fl oz) of the yogurt, the salt and some pepper. Cover the fish mixture with plastic film and return it to the refrigerator.

Bring a saucepan of water to the boil and cook the sliced asparagus until it is tender — 1 to 2 minutes. Pour the asparagus into a colander, refresh it under cold running water and drain it well.

Place the chilled pastry shells on a baking sheet and bake them for 10 minutes. Remove them from the oven and reduce the oven temperature to 180°C (350°F or Mark 4). Divide the asparagus equally among the pastry cases, arranging the pieces neatly in the bottom of each one. Spoon the sole mixture on top of the asparagus, spreading it evenly. Return the tartlets to the oven and cook them until the sole mixture is very lightly set — 6 to 8 minutes.

Remove the tartlets from the oven and set them aside to cool. When they are cold enough to handle, carefully lift them from their tins, place them on a tray and cover with foil. Refrigerate the tartlets until they are well chilled — about 2 hours.

Just before serving, spread the remaining yogurt in a thin layer evenly over the top of each tartlet, arrange strips of smoked salmon around its edges, and sprinkle with the chives.

Serve the tartlets on individual plates, garnished with thinly sliced cucumber.

Phyllo Flowers with a Prawn-Tomato Filling

PAPER-THIN PHYLLO SHEETS, DRAPED OVER MOULDS WITHOUT
OIL OR BUTTER, MAKE LIGHT, CRISP CASES FOR MOIST FILLINGS.

Serves 6
Working time: about 30 minutes
Total time: about 50 minutes

Calories **55**
Protein **5g**
Cholesterol **80mg**
Total fat **1g**
Saturated fat **0g**
Sodium **40mg**

3	sheets phyllo pastry, each about 30 cm (12 inches) square	3
60 g	fromage frais	2 oz
½ tsp	tomato paste	½ tsp
1	garlic clove, crushed	1
¼ tsp	salt	¼ tsp
	freshly ground black pepper	
2	tomatoes, skinned, halved and seeded (page 10)	2
125 g	peeled cooked prawns	4 oz
2 tsp	finely chopped dill or fennel	2 tsp
6	dill or fennel sprigs, for garnish	6

Preheat the oven to 190°C (375°F or Mark 5). Cut the phyllo sheets into 9 cm (3½ inch) squares. Stack the squares and cover them with a cloth to keep them from drying out.

Drape four squares of phyllo over a small brioche or dariole mould, giving the mould a quarter turn after you put on each square so that the points of the squares resemble a flower. Make five more flowers in the same way. Arrange them on a baking sheet and bake them in the oven until the pastry is golden-brown — 6 to 8 minutes.

In a small bowl, combine the *fromage frais* with the tomato paste, the garlic, the salt and some pepper. Set a small strainer over the bowl, place the tomato halves in the strainer and squeeze them gently so their juice falls into the *fromage frais*. Remove the tomato flesh from the sieve and cut it into strips with a sharp knife. Stir the tomato strips and the prawns into the *fromage frais* mixture.

Unmould the phyllo flowers when they have cooled, using a sharp knife to ease the baked pastry gently off the moulds. With a teaspoon, fill the phyllo flowers with the prawn and tomato mixture. Sprinkle them with the chopped dill or fennel and serve immediately, garnished with the sprigs of fennel or dill.

Pears with Prosciutto

Serves 4
Working time: about 15 minutes
Total time: about 25 minutes

Calories **55**		
Protein **3g**	4	ripe pears	4
Cholesterol **10mg**	125 g	curly endive, washed and dried	4 oz
Total fat **5g**	1	bunch watercress, stems removed, leaves washed and dried	1
Saturated fat **1g**			
Sodium **195mg**	4	slices prosciutto (about 60 g/2 oz), halved lengthwise	4

Lemon dressing		
1 tbsp	virgin olive oil	1 tbsp
2 tsp	fresh lemon juice	2 tsp
	freshly ground black pepper	
2 tsp	chopped parsley	2 tsp

To make the dressing, put the olive oil and the lemon juice in a small bowl, stir with a fork to blend thoroughly, and stir in some black pepper and the chopped parsley. Peel, quarter and core the pears, and toss them gently in the dressing to coat them thoroughly. Leave them to steep for 10 minutes.

Arrange the curly endive and the watercress leaves on four serving plates and top them with the prosciutto and the fruit. Sprinkle any remaining dressing over the salad and serve it immediately.

2 *Crêpes prepared with a skimmed-milk batter envelop a piquant filling of crab meat and cucumber, spiked with chopped onion and fresh ginger (recipe, page 83).*

Hot First Courses

For guests who have braved the elements on a cold winter evening to travel to your home, the finest welcome you can provide is a hot hors-d'oeuvre straight from the oven or pan. A parchment packet, slit with a knife, releases the fragrance of the delicacies that have steamed inside it; a soufflé rises golden above the rim of its dish; brochettes of marinated duck sizzle on their plates. Appetite is whetted, conversation aroused, and the evening is already suffused with warmth and enjoyment.

Wintry weather is not the only factor that may lead you to prefer a hot hors-d'oeuvre to a cold one. A light or cold main course invites indulgence in a rich, hot hors-d'oeuvre, such as a warm salad of pigeon breasts that have been steeped in a Madeira-flavoured vinaigrette and tossed with wild mushrooms *(page 110)*. Other filling hors-d'oeuvre include risottos *(pages 72-73)*, shortcrust tartlets and crêpes stuffed with savoury fillings.

A hot hors-d'oeuvre may also precede a substantial hot main course, provided you plan the meal to offer a contrast of ingredients, textures and cooking methods. Before a plain roast, offer a sauced or dressed hors-d'oeuvre, such as asparagus with tarragon dressing *(page 60)* or seafood wonton with mango and ginger sauce *(page 96)*. If the main course is rich or creamy, choose a simple grilled, baked or steamed first course, such as the chicken and mango brochettes on page 109, or the stuffed vine leaves on page 70. If the main course is a complex assemblage of ingredients, select a less elaborate first course, such as the grilled goat cheese rounds on page 81, or the miniature beef meatballs on page 119.

Whichever your final choice, the ingredients and cooking method in every recipe in this chapter have been carefully planned to keep fat, calories and cholesterol low. In addition, step-by-step photographs throughout the chapter illustrate techniques that will expand any cook's repertoire of hors-d'oeuvre. These make light work of the creation of soufflés, the carving of bread cases, the formation of airy mixtures of seafood or poultry into elegant, oval quenelles, and the crafting of Middle-Eastern pastries, Chinese dumplings and other enticing preludes to a meal.

Asparagus with Tarragon Dressing

Serves 4
Working (and total) time: about 20 minutes

Calories **85**
Protein **3g**
Cholesterol **0mg**
Total fat **8g**
Saturated fat **1g**
Sodium **100mg**

500 g	fresh asparagus, stalks trimmed and peeled to about 2.5 cm (1 inch) below the tips	1 lb
1 tbsp	fresh lemon juice	1 tbsp
¼ tsp	salt	¼ tsp
	white pepper	
2 tbsp	virgin olive oil	2 tbsp
1 tbsp	chopped fresh tarragon	1 tbsp

To cook the asparagus, pour water into a large frying pan to a depth of 2.5 cm (1 inch), and bring the liquid to the boil. Line up the asparagus on the bottom of the pan, with all the tips facing in one direction. Position the pan so the thicker ends of the stalks lie over the centre of the heat source. Cook the asparagus until it is tender but still crisp — about 5 to 7 minutes.

While the spears are cooking, make the dressing. Mix together the lemon juice, the salt and some white pepper in a small bowl. When the salt has dissolved, whisk in the olive oil.

With a fish slice, lift the asparagus gently out of the water, place it in a colander and refresh it briefly under cold running water. Drain the asparagus a second time and pat it dry with a clean tea towel. Arrange the spears on individual warmed dishes, spoon the dressing over them and sprinkle with the chopped tarragon.

EDITOR'S NOTE: *Peeling the asparagus ensures that the stalks cook at the same rate as the tender tips.*

Parcels of Spring Vegetables with Lemon Butter

Serves 4
Working time: about 40 minutes
Total time: about 1 hour

Calories **70**
Protein **3g**
Cholesterol **20mg**
Total fat **6g**
Saturated fat **4g**
Sodium **70mg**

16	small young carrots about 9 cm (3½ inches) long, scraped, with about 4 cm (1½ inches) of green tops retained	16
150 g	mange-tout, topped and tailed, strings removed	5 oz
20	thin asparagus spears, trimmed	20
12	spring onions, trimmed and cut into 10 cm (4 inch) lengths	12
½	sweet yellow pepper, seeded, deribbed and cut into thin strips	½
4 tsp	thinly cut chives	4 tsp
4 tsp	chopped fresh chervil	4 tsp
4 tsp	chopped fresh tarragon	4 tsp
Lemon butter		
30 g	unsalted butter, softened	1 oz
1 tsp	grated lemon rind	1 tsp
1 tsp	fresh lemon juice	1 tsp
⅛ tsp	salt	⅛ tsp
	freshly ground black pepper	

In a small bowl, mix together all the ingredients for the lemon butter, cover the bowl with plastic film and place it in the refrigerator to chill. Preheat the oven to 220°C (425°F or Mark 7).

Pour enough water into a saucepan to fill it about 2.5 cm (1 inch) deep. Put a steamer in the pan and bring the water to the boil. Add the carrots, cover them tightly and steam them until they are partially cooked, but still firm — about 8 minutes. Drain them in a colander and transfer them to a large bowl. Toss in the mange-tout, asparagus, spring onions and pepper.

Cut out four circles about 25 cm (10 inches) in diameter from parchment paper. Fold each circle in half, crease the parchment, then open it out. Brush each circle lightly with oil.

Spoon a quarter of the vegetables on to a paper circle, keeping the filling to one side of the crease and forming a neat rectangle lying parallel to the fold. Dot the vegetables with a little lemon butter, sprinkle them with 1 teaspoon of each of the herbs and fold over the other half of the paper to enclose the filling.

Crimp the edges of the paper, in overlapping double folds, until the package is sealed. Fill and seal the remaining three parcels in the same way.

Brush the outside of the packages with a little oil, to prevent the paper from becoming soggy in the oven. Place the parcels on a baking sheet and bake them in the oven for 12 minutes. Serve the sealed packets on individual plates and let the diners pierce and cut open their own parcels to savour the aroma.

Celeriac Timbales with Wild Mushrooms and Madeira Sauce

THE GNARLED CELERIAC, WITH ITS SUBTLE FLAVOUR REMINISCENT OF CELERY, IS AT ITS BEST IN AUTUMN AND WINTER.

Serves 4
Working time: about 35 minutes
Total time: about 1 hour and 10 minutes

Calories **140**
Protein **4g**
Cholesterol **0mg**
Total fat **5g**
Saturated fat **1g**
Sodium **60mg**

500 g	celeriac, peeled, cut into 1 cm (½ inch) cubes	1 lb
2 tsp	fromage frais	2 tsp
1	egg white	1
	freshly ground black pepper	
1 tbsp	walnut oil	1 tbsp
Wild mushroom filling		
12.5 cl	Madeira	4 fl oz
12.5 cl	unsalted chicken stock (recipe, page 9)	4 fl oz
125 g	chanterelles or oyster mushrooms	4 oz
1 tbsp	fromage frais	1 tbsp
¼ tsp	chopped fresh thyme or ⅛ tsp dried thyme	¼ tsp
Madeira sauce		
8 cl	Madeira	3 fl oz
35 cl	unsalted chicken stock (recipe, page 9)	12 fl oz
	small thyme sprigs, for garnish	

Put a little water — about 2.5 cm (1 inch) — in a saucepan, place a steamer in the pan and bring the water to the boil. Steam the celeriac until tender —

about 9 to 10 minutes — and purée it by passing it through a sieve or a food mill. Transfer the purée to a heavy saucepan, and cook it gently for 1 to 2 minutes to evaporate any excess moisture, stirring constantly to prevent it from sticking. Remove the purée from the heat and beat in the *fromage frais*, the egg white and some black pepper. Cover the mixture and chill it for 30 minutes in the refrigerator.

Preheat the oven to 200°C (400°F or Mark 6).

Meanwhile, prepare the mushroom filling. Place the Madeira and the stock in a saucepan, bring them to the boil, and cook them over high heat until the liquid is reduced to 3 cl (1 fl oz). Set aside eight small, un-blemished mushrooms (if the caps are large, break off eight nicely shaped pieces) and chop the remainder finely with a sharp knife. Stir the chopped mushrooms, *fromage frais* and thyme into the stock mixture and set the filling aside to cool.

Brush four 12.5 cl (4 fl oz) ramekin dishes lightly with the walnut oil. Spoon about three quarters of the celeriac purée into the ramekins, pressing it into the sides and bottom of the dish and forming a well in the centre of each one. Spoon the mushroom filling into these hollows, and cover with the remaining purée.

Arrange the ramekins in a deep roasting tin or baking dish, and pour in enough boiling water to come half way up their sides. Bake the ramekins for about 10 minutes, remove them from the oven and set them aside to rest while you prepare the sauce.

In a saucepan, bring the Madeira and the stock to the boil and continue to cook them over high heat until the liquid is reduced to 12.5 cl (4 fl oz). Reduce the heat, add the reserved mushroom caps to the sauce and simmer for about 1 minute.

To unmould the timbales, run a palette knife round the inside edges of the ramekins, and turn them out carefully on to warmed serving plates. If necessary, smooth the surfaces of the timbales with the palette knife. Using a slotted spoon, remove the mushroom caps from the sauce, and place two next to each timbale. Spoon the sauce round the timbales and serve them warm, garnished with the thyme sprigs.

EDITOR'S NOTE: *If chanterelles or oyster mushrooms are unavailable, a mixture of 90 g (3 oz) of button mushrooms and 15 g (½ oz) of dried wild mushrooms, soaked for 20 minutes and drained, may be substituted.*

Steamed Cucumber with Herb and Yogurt Sauce

Serves 4
Working (and total) time: about 20 minutes

Calories **50**
Protein **3g**
Cholesterol **0mg**
Total fat **3g**
Saturated fat **2g**
Sodium **40mg**

1	large cucumber	1
	freshly ground black pepper	
250 g	thick Greek yogurt	8 oz
1 tbsp	chopped fresh dill	1 tbsp
1 tbsp	chopped parsley	1 tbsp
½ tbsp	chopped fresh tarragon	½ tbsp
4	fresh tarragon sprigs	4

With a sharp knife, peel the cucumber and chop it into 2.5 cm (1 inch) pieces. Remove the seeds from the centre of each piece with an apple corer. Pour enough water into a saucepan to fill it about 2.5 cm (1 inch) deep. Set a vegetable steamer in the pan and bring the water to the boil. Place the cucumber pieces in the steamer, season with some black pepper, cover the saucepan and steam until the cucumber is just heated through — 3 to 4 minutes.

While the cucumber is steaming, prepare the sauce by mixing together the Greek yogurt, dill, parsley and chopped tarragon in a small saucepan. Heat the mixture over very low heat until the yogurt is warm, but not hot — about 1 minute.

Using a slotted spoon, transfer the cucumber pieces to warmed plates. Garnish the cucumber with the tarragon sprigs and serve with the warm yogurt sauce.

Baby Baked Potatoes with Celeriac-Watercress Purée

Serves 6
Working time: about 20 minutes
Total time: about 1 hour

Calories **100**
Protein **3g**
Cholesterol **10mg**
Total fat **8g**
Saturated fat **2g**
Sodium **100mg**

6	new potatoes, washed	6
1 tsp	safflower oil	1 tsp
250 g	celeriac, peeled and roughly chopped	8 oz
15 g	unsalted butter	½ oz
60 g	watercress, tough stems removed	2 oz
1 tbsp	thick Greek yogurt	1 tbsp
1½ tbsp	skimmed milk	1½ tbsp
⅛ tsp	salt	⅛ tsp
	freshly ground black pepper	
6	red endive or red lollo lettuce leaves, washed and dried	6
24	lamb's lettuce leaves, washed and dried	24
Vinaigrette dressing		
2 tsp	white wine vinegar	2 tsp
⅛ tsp	salt	⅛ tsp
	freshly ground black pepper	
6 tsp	safflower oil	6 tsp

Preheat the oven to 220°C (425°F or Mark 7).

With a sharp knife, make a shallow slit lengthwise down the centre of each potato. Rub the skins of the potatoes with the oil, and place them on a rack in the oven to bake for 35 to 40 minutes.

While the potatoes are baking, cook the celeriac in a large saucepan of boiling water until it is soft — about 30 minutes. Meanwhile, melt the butter in a non-reactive saucepan and cook the watercress over low heat until it wilts — about 1 minute.

Drain the celeriac in a colander and place it in a food processor or blender together with the watercress, yogurt and milk. Process the mixture until it forms a purée, and season it with the salt and some pepper. Place the purée in a small saucepan and warm it through over very low heat while you make the vinaigrette dressing.

In a small bowl, stir together the vinegar, the salt and some pepper. Blend in the oil.

Arrange the lettuce leaves on a serving platter. Remove the potatoes from the oven, and use a spoon or a knife to open up the central slits a little wider. Place the potatoes on the bed of salad, and spoon the celeriac-watercress purée into the openings in the potatoes. Dribble the vinaigrette over the salad leaves, and serve the potatoes immediately, with any remaining purée on the side.

EDITOR'S NOTE: *For a special occasion, garnish the potatoes with a few spoonfuls of the bright orange salmon roe known as keta, which is available from delicatessens.*

Cutting across the short end of the rectangle, slice the dough into strips about 5 mm (¼ inch) wide.

Fill the pastry-lined tins with the mushroom mixture. Moisten the dough strips with cold water and arrange four of them in a lattice pattern on the top of each tartlet. Press the strips firmly into position, then trim them to fit the tins exactly.

Brush the lattices with the reserved beaten egg to glaze them. Place the tartlets on a baking sheet, and bake until golden-brown — 20 to 25 minutes.

With the aid of a palette or table knife, carefully remove the tartlets from their baking tins and transfer them to heated serving plates. Serve the tartlets hot, sprinkled with the chopped parsley.

Hot Chick-Pea Salad

THE EARTHY SAVOUR OF HOT, FRESHLY COOKED CHICK-PEAS MINGLED WITH THE FRUITY FRAGRANCE OF GOOD-QUALITY OLIVE OIL PRODUCES A SIMPLE BUT AROMATIC SALAD, RICH IN PROTEIN.

Serves 6
Working time: about 20 minutes
Total time: 2 hours and 10 minutes (includes soaking)

Calories **240**
Protein **12g**
Cholesterol **0mg**
Total fat **8g**
Saturated fat **1g**
Sodium **160mg**

350 g	chick-peas, picked over to remove any grit and stones	12 oz
6 tbsp	finely chopped flat-leaf parsley	6 tbsp
2 tbsp	finely chopped fresh oregano	2 tbsp
1	onion, finely chopped	1
	virgin olive oil	
	red wine vinegar	
	salt	
	freshly ground black pepper	

Rinse the chick-peas under cold running water, then put them in a large, heavy-bottomed saucepan and pour in enough cold water to cover them by about 7.5 cm (3 inches). Discard any that float to the surface. Cover the pan, leaving the lid ajar, and slowly bring the liquid to the boil over medium-low heat. Boil the chick-peas for 2 minutes, then turn off the heat and soak them for at least 1 hour. (Alternatively, soak the peas overnight in cold water.) Drain the peas; return them to the pan and cover with at least twice their volume of fresh water. Bring the liquid to the boil, reduce the heat to maintain a strong simmer, and cook the peas until they are tender — about 1 hour.

Meanwhile, combine the parsley and oregano in a small bowl, and put the chopped onion in a second bowl. When the chick-peas are cooked, drain them in a colander, and transfer them to a warmed serving dish. Serve them immediately, accompanied by cruets of oil and vinegar, the bowls of chopped herbs and onion, and the seasonings. The salad can be dressed individually to taste.

Vine Leaves with a Rice and Date Stuffing

VINE LEAVES SERVED HOT WITH A SAVOURY STUFFING ARE
CLASSICS OF EASTERN MEDITERRANEAN CUISINES. THIS
RECIPE INCORPORATES A MEATLESS FILLING.

Serves 4
Working time: about 35 minutes
Total time: about 1 hour

Calories **170**
Protein **5g**
Cholesterol **0mg**
Total fat **2g**
Saturated fat **0g**
Sodium **90mg**

90 g	round-grain brown rice	3 oz
125 g	fresh dates, stoned and chopped	4 oz
1 tbsp	pine-nuts, tossed in a frying pan over medium heat until golden, coarsely chopped	1 tbsp
1	lemon, grated rind and juice of one half, the remainder halved vertically and thinly sliced	1
1 tbsp	chopped parsley	1 tbsp
	freshly ground black pepper	
8	large fresh vine leaves, blanched for a few seconds in boiling water, patted dry	8
Tomato sauce		
1	small onion, chopped	1
250 g	ripe tomatoes, skinned, seeded (page 10) and chopped	8 oz
15 cl	tomato juice	¼ pint
6 tbsp	unsalted chicken stock (recipe, page 9) or water	6 tbsp
⅛ tsp	sugar	⅛ tsp
1	bay leaf	1
1	fresh thyme sprig	1
	freshly ground black pepper	

Bring ½ litre (16 fl oz) of water to the boil in a
saucepan. Boil the rice until it is tender — 25 to 30
minutes. Drain it thoroughly in a colander.

Meanwhile, place all the sauce ingredients in a small
saucepan. Bring the mixture to the boil, cover the pan
and simmer over low heat for 15 minutes. Remove the
bay leaf and the thyme sprig and purée the sauce in a
food processor or blender until it achieves a smooth
consistency. (For an even smoother texture, rub the
purée through a sieve as well.) Preheat the oven to
190°C (375°F or Mark 5).

Put the rice in a bowl and stir in the dates, pine-nuts,
lemon rind and juice, parsley and some pepper. Lay

Mussels in White Wine

Serves 8
Working (and total) time: about 30 minutes

Calories **120**
Protein **13g**
Cholesterol **30mg**
Total fat **5g**
Saturated fat **3g**
Sodium **195mg**

2 kg	mussels, scrubbed and debearded	4 lb
1	onion, chopped	1
3	garlic cloves, crushed	3
2	bay leaves	2
60 g	parsley, finely chopped	2 oz
3	thyme sprigs	3
30 g	unsalted butter	1 oz
	freshly ground black pepper	
¼ litre	white wine	8 fl oz

Place the mussels in a large, heavy-bottomed saucepan with the onions, garlic, bay leaves, parsley and thyme. Add the butter and some pepper, and pour in the white wine. Cover the pan and cook the mussels over high heat, lifting and shaking the pan several times, until the shells have opened — 3 to 5 minutes, depending on the size and number of mussels.

With a slotted spoon, transfer the mussels to individual soup plates, discarding the bay leaves and any mussels that remain closed. Pour the cooking liquid through a strainer into the soup plates, and serve the mussels hot in their broth.

SUGGESTED ACCOMPANIMENT: *crusty bread.*

Steamed Clams with Spinach

Serves 4
Working (and total) time: about 20 minutes

Calories **115**
Protein **9g**
Cholesterol **20mg**
Total fat **4g**
Saturated fat **2g**
Sodium **100mg**

1 tbsp	unsalted butter	1 tbsp
1	onion, finely chopped	1
1	garlic clove, finely chopped	1
12.5 cl	white wine	4 fl oz
1 tbsp	chopped parsley	1 tbsp
½ tsp	freshly ground black pepper	½ tsp
750 g	small clams in their shells	1½ lb
250 g	fresh spinach, washed, stems removed, leaves shredded	8 oz
1	lemon, quartered	1

Melt the butter in a deep, non-reactive saucepan, add the onion and garlic, and cook, stirring continuously, until the onion is soft but not coloured — about 5 minutes. Stir in the wine, parsley and pepper, and bring the mixture to the boil. Add the clams and cook them for 5 minutes, covered, until their shells begin to open. With a slotted spoon, remove the clams from the pan and discard the loose top half of each shell. Place the clams in a warmed dish and cover with a tea towel.

Simmer the spinach in the wine and onion mixture for 2 minutes over moderate heat. When the spinach is cooked, drain it thoroughly in a colander set over a bowl. Press the spinach to drain off any excess liquid. Return the liquid to the pan. Divide the spinach among four plates, and place an equal number of clams on top of each portion.

Bring the reserved pan juices to the boil and cook over high heat for 1 minute to reduce them. Spoon the juices over the clams and spinach, and serve them garnished with the lemon wedges.

EDITOR'S NOTE: *Cockles may be substituted for the clams.*

Sardines in Vine Leaves

Serves 4
Working time: about 15 minutes
Total time: about 1 hour and 15 minutes (includes marinating)

Calories **140**
Protein **8g**
Cholesterol **30mg**
Total fat **11g**
Saturated fat **2g**
Sodium **225mg**

8	small sardines (about 125 g/4 oz each), gutted	8
2 tbsp	virgin olive oil	2 tbsp
1	lemon, juice only	1
1	garlic clove, finely chopped	1
¼ tsp	salt	¼ tsp
8	fresh thyme sprigs, or 1 tsp dried thyme	8
8	fresh oregano sprigs, or 1 tsp dried oregano	8
8	fresh vine leaves, or preserved vine leaves, rinsed	8

Rinse the sardines and pat them dry. In a dish large enough to hold all the fish in a single layer, mix to-gether the olive oil, lemon juice, chopped garlic and salt. Place the fish in the dish, turning them in the marinade. Cover the dish with a lid or plastic film and place in the refrigerator for 1 hour. Turn the sardines once while they are marinating.

Preheat the grill to high. Remove the fish from the marinade and place each one on a vine leaf, together with a sprig of thyme and a sprig of oregano, or a sprinkling of dried thyme and oregano. Roll up the sar-dines in the vine leaves, tuck the ends of the leaves underneath the fish to form secure parcels and place them on the grill rack.

Grill the sardines for 3 minutes on each side, watch-ing carefully to make sure the parcels do not burn. Place two of the wrapped sardines on each plate and serve the fish immediately, to be unwrapped at the table. When the leaves are pulled off, the fish skins and scales will come away with them.

EDITOR'S NOTE: *The technique described for grilling sardines can also be used with small red mullet.*

Oriental Fish Parcels

STEAMING FOOD IN PAPER PACKAGES IS A TECHNIQUE COMMON
TO CHINESE AND OTHER ORIENTAL CUISINES.

Serves 4
Working (and total) time: about 20 minutes

Calories **80**	150 g	carrots, cut into fine julienne	5 oz
Protein **11g**	3	spring onions, cut into fine julienne	3
Cholesterol **35mg**			
Total fat **3g**	2 tsp	chopped fresh coriander	2 tsp
Saturated fat **1g**	300 g	white fish fillet (such as cod, or haddock), skinned	10 oz
Sodium **85mg**	2 tsp	sesame oil	2 tsp
		freshly ground black pepper	
	1	lime, cut into thin wedges, for garnish	1

Cut out four 25 cm (10 inch) squares of greaseproof paper. In a small bowl, mix together the carrot and spring onion strips and the chopped coriander. Divide the mixture of vegetables and herbs equally among the paper squares.

With a sharp knife, slice the fish thinly into strips and divide the strips evenly among the squares. Sprinkle each portion with the sesame oil and some freshly ground black pepper.

Fold a paper square to enclose the fish and vegetables: bring two sides of the square up over the filling, allowing one side to overlap the other. Fold over a margin of about 1 cm (½ inch) on both remaining sides. Fold each of the margins over once again to enclose the packet completely, pressing down on the creases to seal them. Repeat the process to wrap the remaining three parcels. Arrange the fish parcels in a single layer on a steamer rack.

Place the rack over boiling water, cover the pan and steam the fish parcels for 5 minutes. Place each parcel, still wrapped, on a serving dish, and garnish with wedges of lime.

Brill and Leek Croustades

TRADITIONALLY, CROUSTADE CASES ARE SATURATED WITH
BUTTER BEFORE BEING CRISPED IN THE OVEN. HERE THEY ARE
LIGHTLY BRUSHED WITH OIL BEFORE BAKING.

Serves 4
Working (and total) time: about 50 minutes

Calories **200**
Protein **10g**
Cholesterol **10mg**
Total fat **8g**
Saturated fat **1g**
Sodium **300mg**

½	large day-old loaf white bread, crust removed	½
1 tbsp	safflower oil	1 tbsp
125 g	leeks, trimmed cleaned and cut into 1 cm (½ inch) cubes	4 oz
12.5 cl	medium dry white wine	4 fl oz
125 g	skinned brill fillets, cut into strips about 6 cm by 5 mm (2½ by ¼ inch)	4 oz
½ litre	unsalted fish stock (recipe, page 9)	16 fl oz
60 g	fromage frais	2 oz
1 tbsp	finely cut chives	1 tbsp

Cut the bread into four 4 cm (1½ inch) thick slices, about 7.5 cm (3 inches) square, and prepare the croustade cases as demonstrated on the opposite page. While the croustades bake, prepare the filling.

In a saucepan, simmer the leeks in the wine until they are tender and the wine is almost completely evaporated. Place the strips of brill on top of the leeks, pour in the stock, which should just cover the fish, reduce the heat so that the liquid barely moves in the pan and poach the fish for 30 seconds.

Remove the fish from the stock with a slotted spoon and place it in a dish. Transfer the leeks in the same way to a separate heated dish, and cover to keep warm. Boil the stock until it is reduced to 4 tablespoons. Reduce the heat to very low and stir in the *fromage frais*. Lightly fold the brill into the sauce and gently heat through — being careful not to boil.

Place a quarter of the leeks in each croustade, spoon on the brill, sprinkle with the chives and serve.

Meanwhile, poach the salmon fillet pieces in the remaining 15 cl (¼ pint) of fish stock until they turn pale pink — 3 to 5 minutes.

Fill a saucepan with a large quantity of boiling water, plunge in the French beans and boil them until they are cooked but still crunchy — 2 to 5 minutes. Set them aside and keep them warm.

Reheat the fish stock and wine mixture over gentle heat and whisk in the cold margarine cubes to thicken it. Keep the sauce warm while you fill the buns.

Place one portion of the poached salmon fillet in each choux bun and set the pastry lid on top. Toss the French beans in the sauce and serve them alongside the filled buns.

Spiced Crab Puffs

THESE HIGHLY FLAVOURED SEAFOOD PUFFS ARE A MARRIAGE OF CHINESE FLAVOURINGS, SUCH AS GINGER, SOY SAUCE AND FIVE-SPICE POWDER, WITH A LOW-FAT ADAPTATION OF CLASSIC FRENCH CHOUX DOUGH.

Serves 4
Working time: about 30 minutes
Total time: about 55 minutes

Calories **245**
Protein **10g**
Cholesterol **80mg**
Total fat **12g**
Saturated fat **3g**
Sodium **200mg**

1 tbsp	safflower oil	1 tbsp
1	large garlic clove, finely chopped	1
1 tsp	grated fresh ginger root	1 tsp
3	spring onions, chopped	3
100 g	white crab meat, picked over and flaked	3½ oz
1 tbsp	rice vinegar	1 tbsp
1 tsp	low-sodium soy sauce or shoyu	1 tsp
¼ tsp	hot red pepper flakes	¼ tsp
1 tbsp	chopped fresh coriander	1 tbsp
Choux dough		
30 g	polyunsaturated margarine	1 oz
15 cl	skimmed milk	¼ pint
75 g	plain flour	2½ oz
¼ tsp	five-spice powder	¼ tsp
⅛ tsp	cayenne pepper	⅛ tsp
1	egg	1
1	egg white	1

Preheat the oven to 190°C (375°F or Mark 5). To make the choux dough, put the margarine and the milk in a saucepan. Cook over low heat until the margarine melts, then bring the liquid to the boil. Meanwhile, sift the flour, five-spice powder and cayenne pepper on to a sheet of greaseproof paper. Add the spiced flour to the saucepan and stir briskly with a wooden spoon until the mixture is well amalgamated and beginning to draw away from the sides of the pan *(page 75, Steps 1 and 2)*. Remove the pan from the heat.

In a small bowl, lightly beat the egg with the egg white, then add the egg mixture to the dough in the pan, beating it in a little at a time. Using a spoon or a piping bag, drop the dough in eight dollops on to a dampened baking sheet. Bake the choux pastries until they are risen, golden-brown and crisp — 20 to 25 minutes. Turn off the oven.

Make a slit in the side of each puff to allow steam to escape, then return the puffs to the oven to keep warm while you prepare the filling.

Heat the oil in a small, heavy frying pan over medium-high heat. Add the garlic and ginger, and stir-fry for 30 seconds. Add the spring onions and crab meat, and stir-fry for 1 minute. Stir in the vinegar, soy sauce and red pepper flakes, and cook for another 30 seconds. Remove the filling from the heat and stir in the chopped coriander. Spoon about a tablespoon of filling into each puff through the slit you cut. Serve the crab puffs warm.

Warm Skate Salad with Red Pepper Vinaigrette

WARM SALADS, OR *TIÈDE* AS THEY ARE KNOWN IN FRENCH CUISINE, ARE COMPOSED OF FRESHLY COOKED SEAFOOD OR MEAT IN A LIGHT DRESSING. THEY APPEAR WITH INCREASING FREQUENCY ON RESTAURANT MENUS, BUT THEY MAKE AN EXCELLENT ADDITION TO THE REPERTOIRE OF THE HOME COOK, EITHER AS IMPRESSIVE DINNER-PARTY STARTERS, OR AS LIGHT MAIN COURSES FOR FAMILY MEALS.

Serves 6
Working (and total) time: about 45 minutes

Calories **95**
Protein **8g**
Cholesterol **25mg**
Total fat **6g**
Saturated fat **1g**
Sodium **100mg**

500 g	skate wings, skinned	1 lb
30 cl	white wine	½ pint
1	small onion, cut in half	1
1	garlic clove, unpeeled	1
1	small carrot, peeled	1
1	parsley sprig	1
1	fresh thyme sprig	1
1	bay leaf	1
175 g	mange-tout, topped, strings removed	6 oz
Red pepper vinaigrette		
1 tbsp	red wine vinegar	1 tbsp
¼ tsp	salt	¼ tsp
2	sweet red peppers, skinned and sieved (page 11)	2
	freshly ground black pepper	
2 tbsp	virgin olive oil	2 tbsp

Rinse the skate wings well under cold running water. In a large non-reactive frying pan, combine the wine, 1 litre (1¾ pints) of water, the onion, garlic, carrot, parsley, thyme and bay leaf. Bring to the boil, then reduce the heat to medium low and add the skate. Poach the fish until the flesh is opaque and cooked through at the thickest part — about 15 minutes.

While the skate cooks, prepare the red pepper vinaigrette. In a small bowl, combine the wine vinegar with the salt, and stir until the salt dissolves. Stir in the sieved red pepper and some black pepper, then whisk in the oil until the dressing is thoroughly blended.

Lift the poached skate wings from their cooking liquid with a slotted spoon, and transfer them to a plate. Blanch the mange-tout in rapidly boiling water for 30 seconds. Drain and refresh briefly under cold running water, then drain again. Arrange the mange-tout on six serving plates.

As soon as the fish is cool enough to handle, use your finger to lift the flesh, in strips, from the cartilage. Place a portion of skate on each bed of mange-tout. Stir the red pepper vinaigrette well with a fork, and serve it alongside the warm skate

EDITOR'S NOTE: *If the skate wings have not been skinned by the fishmonger, slip a sharp, thin-bladed knife between the skin and the flesh. Pressing the blade of the knife against the skin and working towards the edge of the wing, cut away the skin with short slicing strokes. Turn the wing over and repeat the process to remove the skin from the other side.*

Smoked Haddock in Leek Wrappers

Serves 6
Working time: about 35 minutes
Total time: about 55 minutes

Calories **90**
Protein **10g**
Cholesterol **30mg**
Total fat **4g**
Saturated fat **2g**
Sodium **450mg**

3	large leeks, two outermost layers only, ends trimmed	3
250 g	smoked haddock fillet, all skin and bones removed	8 oz
1	egg	1
4 tbsp	plain low-fat yogurt	4 tbsp
	freshly ground black pepper	
12.5 cl	dry white wine	4 fl oz
1 tbsp	fresh lemon juice	1 tbsp
1	shallot, finely chopped	1
15 g	unsalted butter, cut into small pieces	½ oz
2 tsp	finely cut chives	2 tsp
1 tsp	finely chopped parsley	1 tsp
⅛ tsp	cayenne pepper	⅛ tsp
½	lemon, thinly sliced	½

To prepare the leek wrappers, bring a large saucepan of water to the boil, add the outer leek layers and blanch them for 2 minutes. Drain the layers, refresh them under cold running water, then pat them dry with paper towels. Trim each layer to a neat rectangle 20 by 10 cm (8 by 4 inches), and set the wrappers aside.

Preheat the oven to 220°C (425°F or Mark 7). In a food processor, blend the smoked haddock fillet, egg, yogurt and pepper to create a smooth purée.

Lay out the leek wrappers on a flat surface. Place 2 teaspoons of the smoked haddock filling on the dark green end of each wrapper. Roll up the packages, pressing them slightly to seal in the filling (above).

Arrange the leek rolls seam side down in a shallow baking dish, just large enough to accommodate them comfortably. Pour the wine and lemon juice over the leeks and cover the dish tightly with dampened greaseproof paper. Bake the rolls until the filling is just set — 15 to 20 minutes. Using a slotted spatula, transfer the leek rolls to a warmed platter and keep them hot while you prepare the sauce.

Strain the juices from the baking dish into a small saucepan and add the shallot. Bring the liquid to the boil over high heat and boil it for 1 minute in order to reduce it slightly.

Remove the pan from the heat and briskly stir in the butter, one piece at a time. When all the butter has been incorporated, spoon the sauce over the leek rolls. Add a sprinkling of chives and parsley, and a small pinch of cayenne, to each serving. Garnish the rolls with the lemon slices, and serve.

EDITOR'S NOTE: *Use the biggest leeks you can find to provide the wrappers. The inner parts of the leeks can be reserved for another use.*

Wine-Glazed Red Mullet

Serves 4
Working (and total) time: about 45 minutes

Calories **140**
Protein **13g**
Cholesterol **25mg**
Total fat **6g**
Saturated fat **1g**
Sodium **160mg**

1	large red mullet (about 300 g/ 10 oz), cleaned and filleted but not skinned	1
¼ tsp	salt	¼ tsp
	freshly ground black pepper	
4 tbsp	red wine	4 tbsp
½	small red onion	½
6	pink or black peppercorns	6
2 tbsp	red wine vinegar	2 tbsp
2 tsp	light unrefined granulated sugar	2 tsp
125 g	red grapes, halved and seeded	4 oz
2	small hearts of radicchio, weighing 90 to 125 g (3 to 4 oz) each, quartered	2
1 tbsp	grapeseed or safflower oil	1 tbsp

Remove the fine bones from the centre of the fish fillet with tweezers. Season the skin-free side of each mullet fillet lightly with the salt and some freshly ground pepper, and set them aside.

Put the red wine, onion and peppercorns in a small non-reactive saucepan. Bring the mixture to the boil, lower the heat and simmer gently until the liquid reduces to about 2 tablespoons. With a slotted spoon, remove and discard the onion and the peppercorns. Add the wine vinegar and sugar to the saucepan and cook the mixture over high heat until it reduces to about 2 tablespoons of syrupy glaze.

Preheat the grill.

Set aside 1 teaspoon of the glaze for the salad dressing and coat the skin side of each fillet with half of the glaze from the saucepan, keeping the remainder in the pan. Brush the grill pan and rack with a little oil and arrange the fish fillets on the rack in the pan, skin side upwards.

In a small bowl, whisk together the oil and the reserved teaspoon of glaze to form the salad dressing. Toss the grapes and radicchio quarters in this mixture and place them in a fireproof dish, ready to heat through under the grill.

Grill the red mullet, skin side upwards, 8 to 10 cm (3½ to 4 inches) below the heat source — never allowing the skin to blister — for 3 to 5 minutes. Half way through the grilling process, brush the fillets with the remaining glaze.

When the fish fillets are fully cooked, remove them from the grill and set them aside while you heat through the grape and radicchio salad for about 30 seconds under the grill.

Remove the fish from the grill pan and slice each fillet diagonally into three or four pieces. Arrange the fish pieces on individual plates with the warm salad, and serve immediately.

Squid in a Spanish Sauce

THIS SPANISH DELICACY IS A CLASSIC *TAPA* — ONE OF A
VARIETY OF SMALL DISHES SERVED AS A SNACK WITH A GLASS
OF SHERRY, OR AS A PRELUDE TO AN EVENING MEAL.

Serves 6
Working time: about 25 minutes
Total time: about 1 hour and 10 minutes

Calories **135**
Protein **14g**
Cholesterol **100mg**
Total fat **6g**
Saturated fat **1g**
Sodium **220mg**

2 tbsp	virgin olive oil	2 tbsp
1	onion, halved and sliced thinly	1
750 g	small squid, cleaned, pouches cut into 1.5 cm (¾ inch) slices, small tentacles left whole, large tentacles sliced	1½ lb
2	garlic cloves, chopped	2
12.5 cl	red wine	4 fl oz
4	tomatoes, skinned, seeded (page 10) and chopped	4
1 tbsp	tomato paste	1 tbsp
1	bay leaf	1
1	thyme sprig	1
¼ tsp	salt	¼ tsp
	freshly ground black pepper	
1 tbsp	chopped parsley	1 tbsp
	lemon wedges, for garnish	

Heat the oil in a heavy-bottomed saucepan and fry the
onion until it is softened. Add the squid and the garlic
and cook them for about 4 minutes, turning them occasionally, until the squid is firm and opaque.

Add the wine, tomatoes, tomato paste, bay leaf,
thyme, salt and some pepper. Cover the pan and cook
the squid until it is tender — about 45 minutes.
Remove the bay leaf and the thyme sprig, then stir in
the chopped parsley.

Turn the sauced squid into a serving dish and garnish with the lemon wedges.

SUGGESTED ACCOMPANIMENT: *crusty bread.*

Fish and Tomato Gratins

Serves 4
Working time: about 25 minutes
Total time: about 55 minutes

Calories **135**
Protein **16g**
Cholesterol **50mg**
Total fat **4g**
Saturated fat **1g**
Sodium **160mg**

300 g	plaice fillets, skinned	10 oz
350 g	tomatoes, skinned, seeded (page 10) and chopped	12 oz
1	garlic clove, crushed	1
1 tbsp	chopped fresh basil	1 tbsp
1 tsp	tomato paste	1 tsp
	freshly ground black pepper	
6 tbsp	fromage frais	6 tbsp
2 tsp	fresh lemon juice	2 tsp
2	egg whites	2
3 tbsp	fresh white breadcrumbs	3 tbsp

Preheat the oven to 190°C (375°F or Mark 5). Bring some water to boil in a large pan and poach the plaice for 2 to 3 minutes. Drain the fillets and set them aside.

Mix together the tomatoes, garlic, basil, tomato paste and some pepper. Divide the tomato mixture among four individual gratin dishes.

Using a fork, flake the cooked fish and place it in a bowl with the *fromage frais* and lemon juice. Whisk the egg whites in another bowl until stiff; fold them into the fish mixture. Season with more black pepper.

Spoon the fish mixture over the tomato and sprinkle the breadcrumbs over the fish. Bake the gratins until the filling is heated through and the breadcrumbs are crisp — 25 to 30 minutes. Serve the gratins hot.

EDITOR'S NOTE: *Oat flakes may be used instead of breadcrumbs for topping the gratins. Other white fish fillets, such as sole or haddock, are an alternative to the plaice.*

Courgettes Filled with Crab

Serves 6
Working time: about 30 minutes
Total time: about 1 hour and 10 minutes

Calories **80**
Protein **2g**
Cholesterol **35mg**
Total fat **3g**
Saturated fat **1g**
Sodium **25mg**

6	courgettes, about 125 g (4 oz) each, trimmed, washed and patted dry	6
15 g	unsalted butter	½ oz
1	very small onion, finely chopped	1
15 g	plain flour	½ oz
15 cl	dry white wine	¼ pint
175 g	fresh crab meat	6 oz
1 tbsp	single cream	1 tbsp
1 tsp	fresh lemon juice	1 tsp
¼ tsp	salt	¼ tsp
	freshly ground black pepper	
15 g	fresh white breadcrumbs	½ oz
1	small carrot, finely julienned, for garnish	1

Preheat the oven to 190°C (375°F or Mark 5).

Cut the courgettes in half lengthwise and score the cut sides lightly with the tines of a fork or a sharp knife. Grease a large, shallow ovenproof dish, and place the courgettes in the dish, cut side down. Cover them with aluminium foil and bake the courgettes until they are cooked through — 45 to 50 minutes.

About 15 minutes before the courgettes are ready, melt the butter in a saucepan, then add the onion and cook it gently until it is very soft but not browned — 3 to 4 minutes. Stir the flour into the onion and cook for 1 minute. Gradually stir the wine into the flour and onion roux, then bring the mixture to the boil, stirring all the time until the sauce becomes very thick. Remove the saucepan from the heat, and stir in the crab meat, cream, lemon juice, salt and some pepper.

Preheat the grill.

When the courgettes are cooked, turn them over so the cut sides are uppermost. Divide the crab mixture evenly among the courgettes, spooning it neatly on top of the halves. Sprinkle the breadcrumbs evenly over the top and place the dish under the grill until the crab mixture is heated through and the breadcrumbs are golden-brown. Serve the courgettes hot, garnished with the carrot julienne.

EDITOR'S NOTE: *The courgettes may be stuffed in advance. When you are ready to serve them, top with the breadcrumbs and heat through under a hot grill.*

Quenelles with Rosé Wine Sauce

THE FISH FOR THESE QUENELLES MUST BE WELL CHILLED: THE COLDER THE FISH, THE MORE EASILY IT WILL ABSORB THE *CRÈME FRAÎCHE*, GIVING A BETTER TEXTURE TO THE FINISHED DISH.

Serves 6
Working time: about 45 minutes
Total time: about 2 hours and 30 minutes (includes chilling)

Calories **155**
Protein **4g**
Cholesterol **70mg**
Total fat **8g**
Saturated fat **3g**
Sodium **95mg**

350 g	skinless, boneless whiting fillet, well chilled	12 oz
2	egg whites	2
⅛ tsp	grated nutmeg	⅛ tsp
⅛ tsp	cayenne pepper	⅛ tsp
¼ tsp	salt	¼ tsp
	white pepper	
125 g	crème fraîche	4 oz
175 g	fromage frais	6 oz
Rosé wine sauce		
1 tbsp	safflower oil	1 tbsp
1	shallot, finely chopped	1
175 g	tomatoes, skinned, seeded (page 10) and chopped	6 oz
30 cl	rosé wine	½ pint
2 tbsp	fromage frais	2 tbsp
¼ tsp	salt	¼ tsp
	freshly ground black pepper	

Put the fish, egg whites, nutmeg, cayenne pepper, salt and some white pepper in a food processor and blend to a smooth paste. With the machine still running, add the *crème fraîche* and the *fromage frais*, a little at a time, and process until the ingredients are thoroughly blended. Turn the mixture into a bowl, cover with plastic film, and refrigerate for about 2 hours.

While the fish mixture is chilling, begin the sauce. Heat the oil in a small saucepan and cook the shallot over moderate heat for 30 seconds. Stir in the tomatoes and the wine, bring the mixture to the boil and cook, stirring occasionally, until the liquid is reduced to about 35 cl (12 fl oz) — about 8 minutes.

Remove the wine sauce from the heat and set it aside.

Choose a shallow non-stick pan at least 30 cm (12 inches) in diameter in which to cook the quenelles. Using two large, deep-bowled dessertspoons, shape the fish mixture into 12 quenelles *(box, opposite page)* and place them in the pan. Do not let the quenelles touch one another, or they may stick together as they cook. Pour boiling water slowly down the side of the pan until the quenelles are just covered, and simmer them gently until just firm — about 10 minutes.

While the quenelles are cooking, reheat the sauce over low heat. Stir in 1 tablespoon of the *fromage frais*, the salt and some pepper. In a small bowl, mix 1 tablespoon of the wine sauce with the remaining *fromage frais*. Distribute the rest of the sauce among six heated serving plates.

Using a slotted spoon, lift the quenelles out of the water. Drain them on paper towels. Place two quenelles on each plate. Dribble the reserved blend of sauce and *fromage frais* between and around the quenelles. Draw out the paler sauce with the edge of a spoon to create a marbled effect, and serve.

Chicken and Spinach Quenelles

Serves 4
Working time: about 35 minutes
Total time: about 1 hour and 30 minutes (includes freezing)

Calories **175**
Protein **16g**
Cholesterol **30mg**
Total fat **7g**
Saturated fat **2g**
Sodium **350mg**

175 g	skinned and boned chicken breast, all sinew and tendon removed	6 oz
750 g	spinach, washed and stemmed	1½ lb
2	egg whites	2
½ tsp	salt	½ tsp
	freshly ground black pepper	
175 g	quark	6 oz

Tomato-basil concasse		
4	large tomatoes, blanched for 10 to 15 seconds, skinned, seeded (page 10) and diced	4
6	shallots, finely chopped	6
½	garlic clove, crushed	½
12	large basil leaves, cut into thin strips	12
⅛ tsp	salt	⅛ tsp
	freshly ground black pepper	
½ tbsp	safflower oil	½ tbsp

In a food processor, reduce the chicken breast to a smooth paste — about 1 minute. Blanch the spinach leaves for 1 minute in 4 litres (7 pints) of boiling water.

Golden Quail in a Spaghetti Squash Nest

Serves 4
Working (and total) time: about 45 minutes

Calories **195**
Protein **24g**
Cholesterol **70mg**
Total fat **7g**
Saturated fat **2g**
Sodium **70mg**

1	small spaghetti squash	1
16	cardamom pods	16
¼ tsp	saffron threads, pounded to a powder in a mortar with ⅛ tsp coarse salt	¼ tsp
1 tbsp	honey	1 tbsp
15 cl	muscat wine	¼ pint
4	quail, plucked and drawn, stray quills and pinfeathers plucked out	4
½ tsp	salt	½ tsp
	freshly ground black pepper	
30 g	pine-nuts, toasted in a small, dry frying pan over medium heat until golden	1 oz

Cook the spaghetti squash whole in a large saucepan of boiling water until a skewer or fork can be inserted into it easily — about 30 minutes. While it cooks, prepare the basting liquid for the quail.

Remove the husks from four of the cardamom pods, place the pods in a mortar and grind them to a powder. In a pan, heat the saffron, ground cardamom, honey and wine over low heat until the honey has dissolved.

Season the cavity of each quail with the salt and some pepper. With a pestle or a heavy knife, lightly crush the 12 remaining cardamom pods and place a quarter of the spice inside each bird. Tie the legs of the quail together with string.

Preheat the grill. Place the quail in a fireproof grill pan, and coat them with a little of the basting liquid. Grill the birds for approximately 1 minute on each side 10 to 15 cm (4 to 6 inches) below the heat source, to brown the skin lightly all over. Reduce the heat and cook the birds gently for a further 15 to 20 minutes, basting them frequently and turning them from time to time. Transfer the quail to a dish, cover it with foil, and set aside to rest for 5 minutes.

Place the grill pan over low heat, and deglaze it by pouring in any remaining basting liquid, stirring and scraping the pan to loosen any browned fragments stuck to the base. Spoon the glaze over the quail. Any remaining glaze can be poured over the pine-nuts to enhance their colour.

When the spaghetti squash is cooked, cut it in half lengthwise and scoop out and discard the seeds and loose fibres. Use a fork to twist out the spaghetti-like strands. Place a small mound of the squash on each of four heated serving plates, and set one grilled bird on each nest. Sprinkle the toasted pine-nuts over the quail and serve them hot.

Duck Brochettes with Spiced Wine Sauce

Serves 4
Working time: about 45 minutes
Total time: about 1 hour and 25 minutes (includes marinating)

Calories **210**
Protein **18g**
Cholesterol **70mg**
Total fat **7g**
Saturated fat **2g**
Sodium **125 mg**

350 g	boned duck breasts	12 oz
5 tbsp	red wine	5 tbsp
¼ tsp	salt	¼ tsp
1 tsp	mixed dried herbs, such as oregano, thyme and marjoram	1 tsp
½	small onion, finely chopped	½
125 g	oyster mushrooms, trimmed and wiped	4 oz
½ tsp	virgin olive oil	½ tsp
Red wine sauce		
1 tsp	grated orange rind	1 tsp
2 tbsp	fresh orange juice	2 tbsp
60 g	redcurrant jelly	2 oz
12.5 cl	red wine	4 fl oz
⅛ tsp	cayenne pepper	⅛ tsp

Carefully remove the skin and fat from the duck breasts. Cut the flesh into neat 2.5 cm (1 inch) cubes.

Put the red wine, salt, herbs and onion in a bowl and mix them well. Add the cubed duck flesh, turning the pieces in the marinade until they are evenly coated. Cover the bowl and allow the duck to marinate at room temperature for at least 1 hour, turning the duck pieces occasionally.

Meanwhile, prepare the sauce. Combine the orange rind and juice, redcurrant jelly, wine and cayenne pepper in a small saucepan. Bring the mixture to the boil, stirring constantly, then lower the heat and simmer the sauce gently until it is reduced by about half. Strain the sauce, return it to the pan, cover and keep warm over low heat while you grill the brochettes.

Preheat the grill to high. Remove the duck pieces from the marinade with a slotted spoon, and thread them alternately with the mushrooms on to small skewers. Place the brochettes on the grill rack and brush them with the oil. Grill the brochettes, turning them once, until the duck pieces are tender yet still slightly pink inside — 4 to 5 minutes. Serve the brochettes hot, with the wine sauce on the side.

EDITOR'S NOTE: *Other varieties of mushroom, such as chanterelles, ceps or button mushrooms, can be used in place of the oyster mushrooms.*

Lamb and Mange-Tout Brochettes with Cranberry Sauce

Serves 6
Working time: about 35 minutes
Total time: about 2 hours and 30 minutes
(includes marinating)

Calories **175**
Protein **19g**
Cholesterol **45mg**
Total fat **7g**
Saturated fat **3g**
Sodium **110mg**

375 g	lamb fillet, trimmed of all visible fat	12 oz
2	lemons, finely grated rind only	2
1	garlic clove, peeled	1
1 tsp	salt	1 tsp
½ tsp	ground cardamom	½ tsp
1 tbsp	virgin olive oil	1 tbsp
1 tbsp	chopped parsley	1 tbsp
125 g	mange-tout, strings removed, blanched for 30 seconds and drained	4 oz

Cranberry sauce

125 g	fresh or frozen cranberries	4 oz
30 g	demerara sugar	1 oz
½ tsp	arrowroot	½ tsp

Cut the lamb fillet into four strips lengthwise, then cut each strip into 12 pieces to make forty-eight 2.5 cm (1 inch) cubes. Put the cubes into a bowl.

In a mortar, combine the lemon rind with the garlic and salt. Pound the mixture with a pestle to form a smooth paste. Gradually work in the cardamom, oil and parsley. Toss the lamb well in this marinade to coat the pieces evenly. Cover the lamb and allow it to marinate at room temperature for 2 hours.

While the meat is marinating, make the sauce. Put the cranberries into a saucepan with the sugar and 15 cl (¼ pint) of water and cook gently until the berries are tender — 8 to 10 minutes. Blend the arrowroot with 2 tablespoons of cold water and stir the resulting paste into the cranberries. Bring the mixture to the boil, stirring continuously. When the sauce thickens and clears, reduce the heat. Simmer the sauce gently for 5 minutes, stirring frequently.

Remove the sauce from the heat and let it cool a little, then cover the surface of the sauce closely with plastic film and set it aside until you are ready to serve the lamb brochettes.

Fifteen minutes before serving, preheat the grill to high. Wrap a mange-tout pod round each piece of lamb and thread four of the wrapped cubes on to each of 12 small skewers, arranging them so the mange-tout wrappers lie on alternating sides of the cubes. Grill the brochettes on a rack, turning them over half way through cooking, until the lamb is cooked yet still slightly pink inside — 3 to 4 minutes. Meanwhile, reheat the sauce over low heat.

Serve the brochettes on preheated individual plates with a little cranberry sauce on the side.

EDITOR'S NOTE: *Instead of cranberry sauce, the brochettes may be served with lemon wedges.*

Prosciutto, Mange-Tout and Tomato Croustades

Serves 4
Working (and total) time: about 1 hour

Calories **140**	½	large day-old loaf white bread	½
Protein **6g**	1 tbsp	safflower oil	1 tbsp
Cholesterol **15mg**	5 tsp	dry sherry	5 tsp
Total fat **7g**	45 cl	unsalted chicken stock (recipe, page 9)	¾ pint
Saturated fat **2g**	½ tsp	herb or Dijon mustard	½ tsp
Sodium **350mg**	60 g	mange-tout, strings removed, cut diagonally in half	2 oz
	175 g	ripe tomatoes, skinned, seeded (page 10) and chopped into 5 mm (¼ inch) cubes	6 oz
	60 g	prosciutto, trimmed of all fat and finely shredded	2 oz
	7 g	unsalted butter, chilled and cut into cubes	¼ oz

Trim off the crust from the bread and cut it into four 4 cm (1½ inch) thick slices, about 7.5 cm (3 inches) square. Prepare the croustade cases as on page 95, Steps 1 to 3. Brush with the oil and bake as in Step 4.

In a small saucepan, boil the sherry over high heat until it is reduced to about 2 teaspoons. Stir in the stock and boil the liquid until it is reduced to about 10 cl (3½ fl oz). Add the mustard, lower the heat and keep the liquid warm while you prepare the filling.

Steam the mange-tout for about 1½ minutes, then drain them in a colander. Reserve eight mange-tout for garnish and transfer the remainder to a bowl. Add the tomatoes and prosciutto, and toss them lightly.

Reduce the heat under the saucepan to very low, and swirl in the cold butter cubes to thicken the sauce. Remove the pan from the heat.

Divide the mange-tout, prosciutto and tomato mixture among the four croustades, spoon the sauce over the croustades, and serve warm, garnished with the reserved mange-tout pieces.

Hors-d'Oeuvre in the Microwave

In the creation of hors-d'oeuvre, the microwave oven is an invaluable ally to the busy cook seeking first-rate results. Not every dish is improved by microwaving: food that needs fast boiling, recipes with many steps and gratins requiring intense heat to form a crust are better cooked conventionally. But others lend themselves particularly well to this new way of cooking. Vegetables display hidden depths of subtlety and savour. Fish and shellfish retain a delicacy and juiciness often lost when treated in more orthodox ways. Fresh herbs do not fade or blacken. Spices such as yellow mustard seeds remain bright and vibrant.

Capitalizing on these advantages of the microwave, the collection of recipes that follows emphasizes simplicity: rich sauces and calorie-laden garnishes become superfluous when foods look appealing and taste so deliciously of themselves.

Things happen faster in a microwave, and many of these recipes are cooked in moments. The bacon-stuffed mushrooms on page 137, for example, need only about 5 minutes to cook, and the artichokes on page 134 only 16 to 20 minutes — less than half the time they would take if boiled on top of the stove.

But to a cook in the throes of dinner party preparations, the most alluring of the microwave's advantages may be its efficiency. With the first course under way in the microwave, the stove is completely free for the rest of the menu. And at the end of the evening comes a final blessing: less washing up. The dish in which the food is assembled and microwaved is often the same one in which it comes to the table.

Some of the recipes in this chapter call for food to be covered with plastic film: make sure that you use only film labelled microwave-safe. If covering a dish containing liquid, leave a corner of the film open, or slit the film with a knife, in order to prevent a dangerous build-up of steam.

The recipes have been tested in 650-watt and 700-watt ovens; the term "high" is used to indicate full power. Remember that food continues to cook after removal from the microwave; be sure to let it stand for a few minutes before you test it for doneness.

Golden Pasta with Chanterelles

Serves 6
Working time: about 45 minutes
Total time: about 2 hours

Calories **185**
Protein **6g**
Cholesterol **45mg**
Total fat **6g**
Saturated fat **2g**
Sodium **60mg**

175 g	strong plain flour	6 oz
30 g	coarsely ground semolina	1 oz
1	egg	1
¼ tsp	saffron threads, pounded to a powder with a pinch of coarse salt in a mortar and dissolved in 2 tbsp of hot water	¼ tsp
2 tsp	yellow mustard seeds	2 tsp
175 g	chanterelle mushrooms	6 oz
Saffron dressing		
	small pinch saffron	
⅛ tsp	coarse salt	⅛ tsp
3 tbsp	crème fraîche or thick soured cream	3 tbsp
5 tbsp	fromage frais	5 tbsp

To prepare the dough in a food processor, sift the flour and semolina into the bowl, add the egg and process the mixture until it forms fine crumbs — about 30 seconds. With the processor switched on, pour in the saffron water a little at a time and process the dough until it forms a ball. To make the pasta dough by hand, sift the flour and semolina into a bowl, make a well in the centre, and add the egg and saffron water. Slowly incorporate the flour mixture into the liquid with a fork. If the dough is sticky, add a teaspoon more flour; if crumbly, add a few drops of water. Knead the dough on a floured surface until it is very smooth and elastic — about 10 minutes.

Let the dough rest for about 30 minutes — or for 1 hour if you have prepared it by hand.

To cut the pasta, divide the dough into four pieces, and roll them out thinly on a floured work surface. Dust each rolled-out piece lightly with flour, pile up the pieces in a single neat stack, and cut the dough into very thin strips with a sharp knife or pastry cutter. Alternatively, roll out the dough and cut it into ribbons with a pasta machine. Hang the pasta over a rolling pin or a broom handle to dry for about 30 minutes.

Place the mustard seeds in a small bowl, and microwave them on high for about 2 minutes to release their aromatic oil. Remove the seeds from the microwave and crush them with a pestle.

▶

Bring 1.25 litres (2 pints) of water to the boil in a large saucepan. Meanwhile, place the chanterelle mushrooms in a dish greased with safflower oil. Cover them with plastic film left slightly open at one side and microwave on high for 2 minutes, turning the dish half way through cooking.

To make the dressing, pound the saffron in a mortar with the salt, mix it with the *crème fraîche* and *fromage frais*, and place in the microwave on high until it is warmed through — about 30 seconds.

Put the pasta in the boiling water and cook it until it is *al dente* — about 2 minutes. Drain thoroughly in a colander, rinse with hot water to remove all excess starch, and then drain thoroughly a second time.

Place the pasta in a large, warmed bowl. Toss it quickly with the saffron dressing, the crushed mustard seeds and the mushrooms, and serve hot.

EDITOR'S NOTE: *Tiny golden oyster mushrooms may be used instead of chanterelles. To cook them, place the mushrooms in a single layer in a round dish lined with kitchen paper, cover with plastic film left slightly open at one side and microwave on high for 1 minute, turning the dish after 30 seconds. Remove the mushrooms from the microwave and leave them to rest, still on the kitchen paper, for another minute.*

Baby Beetroots in Orange and Walnut Dressing

Serves 4
Working time: about 30 minutes
Total time: about 45 minutes

Calories **105**
Protein **2g**
Cholesterol **0mg**
Total fat **9g**
Saturated fat **1g**
Sodium **40mg**

6	small beetroots (about 350g/12 oz), carefully scrubbed clean but unpeeled	6
1 tbsp	walnut oil	1 tbsp
1 tbsp	safflower oil	1 tbsp
2 tbsp	fresh orange juice	2 tbsp
1 tsp	grated orange rind	1 tsp
15g	shelled walnuts, finely chopped	½ oz
	freshly ground black pepper	
90 g	curly endive	3 oz
1	onion, sliced into thin rings	1

Put the beetroots into a casserole and add hot water to reach half way up the beetroots. Cover the casserole and microwave on high for 10 minutes. Using a spoon, turn the beetroots over, then replace the lid and continue microwaving until the beetroots are just tender — about 7 minutes more.

Remove the beetroots from the casserole with a slotted spoon and leave them to cool while you make the dressing. In a small bowl, beat together the walnut oil, safflower oil, orange juice, grated orange rind, chopped walnuts and some pepper.

When the beetroots are cool enough to handle, peel them with a sharp knife. Divide the curly endive among four plates. Cut the beetroots into thin rounds and arrange them, together with the onion rings, on top of the beds of curly endive leaves.

Stir the dressing rapidly with a fork and pour it over the beetroot slices and onions, making sure that the walnuts are evenly distributed.

Scorzonera with Walnuts and Chervil

BLACK-SKINNED SCORZONERA AND ITS PALER RELATIVE,
SALSIFY, HAVE A DELICATE FLAVOUR SAID BY SOME TO
RESEMBLE THAT OF THE OYSTER. INDEED, SALSIFY IS SOMETIMES
KNOWN AS OYSTER-PLANT.

Serves 4
Working time: about 35 minutes
Total time: about 2 hours (includes chilling)

Calories **140**
Protein **2g**
Cholesterol **0mg**
Total fat **12g**
Saturated fat **2g**
Sodium **130mg**

3 tbsp	fresh lemon juice	3 tbsp
½ tsp	salt	½ tsp
500 g	scorzonera or salsify, scrubbed well and cut into 5 cm (2 inch) lengths	1 lb
2 tbsp	safflower oil	2 tbsp
1 tsp	finely chopped parsley	1 tsp
2 tbsp	torn fresh chervil	2 tbsp
	freshly ground black pepper	
2 tbsp	shelled walnuts, chopped	2 tbsp

In a deep bowl, combine 1 tablespoon of the lemon juice and ¼ tsp of the salt with 45 cl (¾ pint) of water. Add the scorzonera, cover the bowl with plastic film, leaving a corner open, and microwave on high until the scorzonera is just fork tender — about 10 minutes.

Drain the scorzonera in a colander, cover the colander with plastic film and let the vegetable rest for 5 minutes to finish cooking in its own steam. Remove the plastic film and set the scorzonera aside to cool.

Meanwhile, prepare the dressing. In a small bowl, mix the oil with the remaining lemon juice, the parsley and the chervil, stirring well until they are thoroughly combined. Season this mixture with the remaining salt and a some freshly ground pepper.

When the scorzonera is cool enough to handle, peel the dark skin from each piece with a sharp knife and place the peeled segments in a deep serving dish. Pour half of the lemon dressing over the scorzonera and set the rest aside.

Let the scorzonera cool to room temperature, cover it with plastic film and place it in the refrigerator to chill for about 1 hour. Just before serving, mix the chopped walnuts into the reserved dressing and spoon it over the chilled scorzonera.

EDITOR'S NOTE: *The scorzonera can also be served warm. While the vegetable cooks, combine all the ingredients for the dressing and mix in the walnuts. As soon as the scorzonera is cool enough to handle, peel it quickly, place it in a deep serving dish, spoon over the walnut dressing and serve the vegetable immediately.*

Stuffed Artichokes

BREADCRUMB-STUFFED ARTICHOKES APPEAR OFTEN IN SICILIAN
AND SOUTHERN ITALIAN COOKERY. ARTICHOKES NOT ONLY COOK
FASTER IN THE MICROWAVE BUT ALSO RETAIN A FRESHER, GREENER
COLOUR THAN WHEN STEAMED ON THE STOVE.

Serves 4
Working time: about 40 minutes
Total time: about 1 hour

Calories **210**
Protein **10g**
Cholesterol **15mg**
Total fat **12g**
Saturated fat **4g**
Sodium **295mg**

125 g	fresh wholemeal breadcrumbs	4oz
4	artichokes	4
1½ tbsp	fresh lemon juice	1½ tbsp
4 tbsp	finely grated Parmesan cheese	4 tbsp
2 tbsp	virgin olive oil	2 tbsp
2	cloves garlic, crushed	2
2 tbsp	finely chopped parsley	2 tbsp
	freshly ground black pepper	

Spread the breadcrumbs for the stuffing in a shallow
layer on a plate and microwave, uncovered, on high
until they start to crisp — 3 to 4 minutes. Set the
crumbs aside while you prepare the artichokes.

Discard the artichoke stalks, cutting them level with
the base so that the artichokes stand upright. With a
small, sharp knife, trim away about 1 cm (½ inch) from
the tips of all the pointed leaves, and slice off about 2.5
cm (1 inch) from the top of each artichoke. Once cut,
artichokes quickly lose their colour when exposed to
the air; keep them green by dipping each one in water
acidulated with 1 tablespoon of the lemon juice.

To cook the artichokes, measure 30 cl (½ pint) water
and the remaining lemon juice into a dish that will
be large enough to hold the artichokes compactly.
Microwave the liquid, uncovered, on high until it

Picture Credits

Cover: Martin Brigdale. 4: top, John Elliott; middle, Chris Knaggs; bottom, Chris Knaggs. 5: top, Jan Baldwin; middle, Chris Knaggs; bottom, Grant Symon. 6: Chris Knaggs. 10-11: John Elliott. 12-13: Chris Knaggs. 14-17: Martin Brigdale. 18: Jan Baldwin. 19: Philip Modica. 20: Chris Knaggs. 21-22: Grant Symon. 23: Philip Modica. 24: Graham Kirk. 25: Chris Knaggs. 26: top, John Elliott; bottom, James Murphy. 27: top, John Elliott; bottom, Martin Brigdale. 28: Chris Knaggs. 29: Tom Belshaw. 30: Philip Modica. 31: Tom Belshaw. 33: John Elliott. 34-35: Tom Belshaw. 36: Chris Knaggs. 37: James Murphy. 38: Tom Belshaw. 39: John Elliott. 40: James Murphy. 41: John Elliott. 42: Martin Brigdale. 43: top, John Elliott; bottom, Chris Knaggs. 44: James Murphy. 45: Graham Kirk. 46: Jan Baldwin. 47-49: Chris Knaggs. 50: Martin Brigdale. 51: Tom Belshaw. 52: Chris Knaggs. 53: Jan Baldwin. 54: Grant Symon. 55: Graham Kirk. 56: James Murphy. 57: Tom Belshaw. 58-59: Martin Brigdale. 60: John Elliott. 61: Martin Brigdale. 62: James Murphy. 63: Grant Symon. 64-65: Chris Knaggs. 66: James Murphy. 67: John Elliott. 68-69: Chris Knaggs. 70-71: John Elliott. 72-73: Chris Knaggs. 74-76: John Elliott. 77: Martin Brigdale. 78: Philip Modica. 79: Grant Symon. 80: Philip Modica. 81: Tom Belshaw. 82: Chris Knaggs. 83: Jan Baldwin. 84: John Elliott. 85: Philip Modica. 86: Chris Knaggs. 87: James Murphy. 88: Chris Knaggs. 89: Tom Belshaw. 90: Chris Knaggs. 91: Tom Belshaw. 92: Chris Knaggs. 93: John Elliott. 94: Tom Belshaw. 95: top, John Elliott; bottom, Martin Brigdale. 96: John Elliott. 97: Chris Knaggs. 98: Jan Baldwin. 99: John Elliott. 100: Grant Symon. 101: James Murphy. 102: Tom Belshaw. 103: Philip Modica. 104: John Elliott. 105: Graham Kirk. 106-108: John Elliott. 109: Tom Belshaw. 110: Chris Knaggs. 111: Martin Brigdale. 112: Chris Knaggs. 113: Jan Baldwin. 114: James Murphy. 115: John Elliott. 116: Martin Brigdale. 117: Chris Knaggs. 118: John Elliott. 119: Martin Brigdale. 120-122: John Elliott. 123: Jan Baldwin. 124: John Elliott. 125: Tom Belshaw. 127: John Elliott. 128: Chris Knaggs. 129: John Elliott. 130: James Murphy. 132-139: Chris Knaggs.

Props: the editors wish to thank the following outlets and manufacturers; all are based in London unless otherwise stated. 12, 13: napkins, Ewart Liddell. 14: marble, W.E. Grant & Co. (Marble) Ltd.; bowl *(centre, back)*, Birgit Blitz, Gruiten, Germany. 17: plate *(right)*, Andrew McGarva, The Craftsmen Potters Shop. 19: small bowl and plate, Winchcombe Pottery, The Craftsmen Potters Shop; large bowl, Tony Gant, The Craftsmen Potters Shop. 21: Formica, Newcastle, Tyne and Wear. 25: marble, W.E. Grant & Co. (Marble) Ltd. 26: plate, Royal Worcester, Worcester. 30: under plate, Villeroy & Boch. 37: plate, Royal Worcester, Worcester. 39: platter, Thomas (London) Ltd. 41: plates, Rosenthal (London) Ltd. 42: platter, Thomas (London) Ltd.; 43: cutlery, Mappin & Webb Silversmiths. 46: plates, Inshop. 47: napkin, Kilkenny. 48: plate, Line of Scandinavia. 58, 59: plates, Villeroy & Boch; cutlery, Mappin & Webb Silversmiths; flower holder, Rosenthal (London) Ltd. 61: plate, Rosenthal (London) Ltd. 64: small bowl, Winchcombe Pottery, The Craftsmen Potters Shop; plate, Tony Gant, The Craftsmen Potters Shop. 65: plates, Chinacraft (Bond St.). 66: bowl, Winchcombe Pottery, The Craftsmen Potters Shop. 68: Formica, Newcastle, Tyne and Wear. 70: bowl, plate and platter, Villeroy & Boch; cutlery, Mappin & Webb Silversmiths. 71: plate, Inshop; place mat, Ewart Liddell. 78: cutlery, Mappin & Webb Silversmiths. 81: cutlery, Next Interior. 82: plates, Hutschenreuther (U.K.) Ltd.; cloth and napkin, Next Interior. 83: lace cloth, Laura Ashley. 89: Formica, Newcastle. 91: plate, Thomas (London) Ltd. 93: plates, David Mellor. 97: cutlery, Mappin & Webb Silversmiths. 98: pink cloth, Next Interior. 99: under plate, Fortnum & Mason; plates, Royal Worcester, Worcester. 100: plates, Villeroy & Boch; cutlery, Mappin & Webb Silversmiths. 102: plate, Villeroy & Boch. 103: plate and bowl, Kilkenny; napkin, Ewart Liddell. 104: tablecloth, Kilkenny. 105: plate, Rosenthal (London) Ltd. 106: plate, Royal Worcester, Worcester. 107: cloth, Next Interior; cutlery, Mappin & Webb Silversmiths. 110: plates, Rosenthal (London) Ltd.; forks, Mappin & Webb Silversmiths; napkins, Next Interior. 111: plates, Villeroy & Boch. 112: Formica, Newcastle. 115: place mat, Ewart Liddell; fork, Next Interior; plates, Thomas (London) Ltd. 116: cloth, Liberty & Co. 122: plate, Royal Worcester, Worcester; napkin and cloth, Kilkenny; small bowl, Rosenthal (London) Ltd. 128, 131: marble, W.E. Grant & Co (Marble) Ltd. 137: plate, Winchcombe Pottery, The Craftsmen Potters Shop; marble, W.E. Grant & Co. (Marble) Ltd.; place mat, Ewart Liddell. 139: fish servers, Mappin & Webb Silversmiths; napkin and cloth, Ewart Liddell.

Acknowledgements

The index for this book was prepared by Myra Clark, London. The editors also wish to thank: Rachel Andrew, London; David Barrett, London; René Bloom, London; Andrew Cameron, London; Nora Carey, Paris; Sean Davis, London; Clare Ferguson, London; Rod Howe, London; Isabella Kranshaw, London; Brian Leonard, London; Paul Moon, London; Christine Noble, London; Oneida, London; Philomena O'Neill, London; Osborne & Little, London; Katherine Reeve, London; Sharp Electronics (UK) Ltd, London; Jane Stevenson, London; Toshiba (UK) Ltd, London; Paul van Biene, London.

Colour Separations by Fotolitomec, S.N.C., Milan, Italy
Typesetting by G. Beard & Son Ltd., Brighton, Sussex, England
Printed and bound by Wing King Tong, Hong Kong.